A Rabbi's Bible

A Rabbi's Bible

Jonathan Magonet

SCM PRESS

London
1991

British Library Cataloguing in Publication Data

Magonet, Jonathan *1942–*
  A Rabbi's Bible.
  1. Bible. Scriptures
  I. Title
  220

ISBN 0–334–02506–0

First published 1991

by SCM Press Ltd
26–30 Tottenham Road London N1 4BZ

Typeset at The Spartan Press Ltd, Lymington, Hants
and printed in Great Britain by
Clays Ltd, St Ives plc, Bungay, Suffolk

For Dorothea,
Gavriel and Abigail
with all my love.

CONTENTS

PREFACE

As a teenager I joined the Junior Membership of the West London Synagogue and rose through the ranks (not particularly difficult in a voluntary organization) to become Chairman. It was the privilege of the 'youth' to conduct the service in the Synagogue once a year on the festival of Hanukah, and the Chairman gave the sermon. I did it with all the religious enthusiasm, commitment and certainty that only a teenager can muster. It was well received and afterwards talking with the Senior Minister, Rabbi Dr Van der Zyl, I generously offered my services to preach whenever he wanted to call on me. He gave me his knowing smile and gently said, 'Yes, we all have *one* sermon inside us!'

Perhaps we all have one book in us as well. I have waited almost twenty years to write this one – twenty years of teaching Rabbinic students at Leo Baeck College, London, Christian audiences in England and Germany, and a variety of people in other contexts and countries. In such a period one acquires a string of anecdotes, favourite passages and examples that only need the opportunity of a little space and time to come crowding out on to the stage. Finding out what I wanted to say with them took a bit longer, but it came with the writing.

For providing that 'space and time' I am grateful to Leo Baeck College for finally forcing me to take a twice postponed sabbatical and ensuring I had the financial support and technical equipment to make full use of it. The bulk of the book was completed while I was the first incumbent of the 'Scholar in Residence Jewish Education Fellowship' of the Unit for Jewish Education, Tel Aviv University and the Department of Education and Culture of the World Zionist Organization for the year 1990. (The title alone deserves a chapter to explain it.) I am particularly grateful to Drs David Zisenwine and David Schers of the Unit of Jewish Education, Dr Hank Skirball, head of the Department of Education and Culture of the WZO, and Asher Amir, Leo Baeck College's 'man in Israel', for all their efforts in arranging it. For additional travel funding I must thank the Sherman Award granted by the Anglo-Jewish Association.

I owe a particular debt of gratitude to Harvey and Ruth Cohen for making their flat available to me throughout my time at Tel Aviv and being supportive in so many other ways.

A number of the latter chapters in the book appeared in a slightly different form in *The Month*, and I am grateful for their permission to reproduce them.

But above all I must thank my wife Dorothea and my children Gavriel and Abigail for giving me the freedom to abandon them for several long months while I got on with the job – and for putting up with my occasional mental absences when I was back home with them tidying it up. Without their understanding and agreement, nothing would have been possible.

The book is dedicated to them, but also to the memory of some of my Bible teachers who are no longer able to share it with me:

Dr Ellen Littmann
Rav Shmuel Sperber
Dr Sara Kamin.

PART ONE

Learning How to Read

1

'Who is this and where is he?'
(Esther 7.5)

There are already too many books about the Bible – as the Bible itself suggests in its own subversive way (Eccles. 12.12). So why another? Well partly because I think I might be able to say some old things in a new way. Partly because I get so irritated by certain other books on the Bible that I want to offer something different.

Among the styles of popular writing on Bible that rankle the most I would include: the pious, breathy enthusiasm of the 'true believer' for whom everything is amazingly new, absolutely true and incredibly significant; closely followed by the ironic, tongue-in-cheek detachment of the media person, who is 'putting over' the latest views on the Bible in much the same way as for any other TV topic ('I am standing now on the very spot where, if archaeologists are to be believed, . . .'). I also get a bit impatient with scholarly colleagues who manage to make a fascinating subject singularly boring.

However, as a selective believer, an occasional media person and a fairly full-time academic myself, I am just as likely to fall into any or all of these traps. So I hope I have now built into this book a device to remind me of these potential sins. As I will repeatedly suggest, the Bible is a subversive book and demands from its commentators no less self-criticism and self-awareness.

Since this is to be a personal book on how one particular Rabbi reads the Bible, it needs a brief personal introduction. Parts of my autobiography will emerge throughout this first section. As a Bible scholar I am largely self-taught. This is not to ignore the great debt I owe to my teachers at Leo Baeck College where I trained as a Rabbi, or at the Hebrew University in Jerusalem where I did research for a PhD that I completed in Heidelberg. Or indeed to a myriad other friends and teachers over the years. But I came late to

Bible studies and it was only a small part of my initial Rabbinic studies, so I did not follow the more conventional route through the maze of biblical disciplines available at University. This has given me a rich but idiosyncratic biblical 'culture'. The result is that I have picked up all sorts of bits and pieces of biblical information over the years from a great number of different sources. This sometimes creates a great muddle, but in the end leads to a very personal synthesis.

I have always enjoyed writing and have had a minor talent for composing songs and poems. I think that has given me an intuition about biblical poetry and narrative that determined the direction of my scholarly career. When I did my PhD in the middle of the seventies on the literary structure of the Book of Jonah, there was very little work done in that particular field. Every step was in the nature of a discovery that then had to be justified by some pretty rigorous argument. It is hard to remember how new it was at the time since the literary analysis of biblical narrative has become a 'growth industry' in the last decade with books, series and scholars abounding.

I came to understand the importance for me of the Hebrew Bible very gradually. The main starting point was as part of my professional studies to become a Rabbi. This may seem obvious, but it is not necessarily so in the Jewish world today. The more traditional Jewish centres of learning, the *yeshivot*, focus more on the later texts like the Talmud, the great compendium of Jewish religious and legal debate that spans the first seven centuries of the common era. The other 'liberal' Rabbinic seminaries in America, until quite recently, were still coming to terms with the great 'scientific' studies of the Bible of the last century and in a way continued that 'tradition' in their concern with finding an 'objective' historical understanding. Leo Baeck College, when I was a student, was relatively new as an institution, so it reflected in a quite dramatic way the search for a new role for Jewish learning, and indeed the Rabbinate itself, in the post-war period. The academic rigour of the scientific approach was important because it still seemed possible to reach some objective conclusions about the history of the texts before us. But the results seemed to do little to nourish the soul of a Jewish world still deeply shaken by the horrors of the *Shoah* (Holocaust). Somehow the Bible had to become again a source of comfort and challenge and religious growth, without sacrificing the seriousness and, indeed, the important results of the scientific approach.

I only appreciate now how far these tensions were acting on us, and I value even more what my teacher Dr Ellen Littmann was trying to do as she sought in her own way to find this new middle path.

A product of the great liberal Jewish seminary in Berlin, the Hochschule, her actual training was in history. She survived the war in Palestine, where she had to work scrubbing floors to make a living. When Leo Baeck College was started, Rabbi Dr Van der Zyl, the real founding father of the College, brought her over to teach Bible. She did this with great dedication and love, particularly for her students who were her only family here, but suffered deeply from the frustration of trying to communicate in what was for her her third language. It was undoubtedly her influence that set me on my professional career in Bible.

But a number of other factors must also have played a part in forming the particular consciousness I have about the Bible. My first studies were in medicine, the family 'business', which it was assumed I would enter. I cannot say that I enjoyed them – there was too much rote learning in my day and not enough encouragement to explore the logical relationships of the information we were acquiring. But having a scientific discipline behind me made me highly critical when I came into the field of biblical studies. Too much of it was merely the repetition of what someone had posited over a century ago and too many hypotheses had taken on the nature of a dogma that could not be criticized. If the same approach had been present in medicine we would still be using leeches and the patient would long since have died. Curiously enough the analogy that frequently came to my mind was that of pathology. Too much of scholarship seemed to be concerned with disinterring and dissecting a dead body rather than engagement with the wonder of a living organism. (My prejudices are already beginning to emerge.)

Another source of my own particular interest was growing up in a household where my father brought home with him some of the stories that came up in his work as a medical hypnotist. He had come to England from Canada during the war to join the Royal Army Medical Corps. As an outsider he never got the chance to enter the mainstream teaching hospital circuit after the war, though I think he was an outstanding clinician. Instead he became a general practitioner, but began to experiment with hypnosis which he had learnt as a medical student in the United States. Since all such unconventional disciplines were considered taboo in the conservative medical establishment of the time, he went his own stubbornly independent way and built up a large private practice. He had a superb intuition about the needs of the patients who came to him, usually after everything else had failed, and a degree of scepticism about the limitations of conventional medical wisdom. But I am sure it was the stories he told, the analysis of what was going on in people's lives that had led to their particular psychosomatic disorders, that impressed upon me the importance of learning how to read between the lines – something to which I will return in chapter 2. I think that his 'holistic' approach (the word was not yet in fashion at the time) gave me a feeling for examining the totality of a 'story', and the need to find its internal integrity – how did it all hold together. Such an approach flew in the face of the conventional biblical scholarship of most of this century that was 'atomistic', splitting up passages into ever smaller components, each of a different historical origin. Not that such an approach is illegitimate, but all too often it seemed to me to be based on dubious criteria and enormous projections into the text of alleged contemporary social or political movements, for which there seemed to be little if any evidence. From my father I gained a love of stories, and a healthy scepticism.

I have to note in passing the degree to which a sense of humour, and certainly of irony, also seems to have been part of my personal development and ultimately of my approach to the Bible. There is a lot of humour in the Bible – but again, until very recently, nobody seemed to notice it or consider it appropriate to draw attention to it (scholars no less than clerics). Granted there are very few belly laughs (with the possible exception of the grotesque death of Eglon (Judg. 3.16–22)!) but there is enormous wit, folk-humour and above all irony throughout. I owe to Rabbi Dr Albert Friedlander the recognition of a certain gallows humour in the story of the Crossing of the Re(e)d Sea. The children of Israel are standing before the waters, Pharaoh's army is on their heels, they turn to Moses and say (presumably in a broad Brooklyn accent to help get the intonation right):

> There weren't enough graves in Egypt that you brought us *here* to die in the wilderness?! (Ex. 14.11)

I mention this because there will be some humour in this book (I hope) and it seems important to indicate its legitimacy both as a biblical mode itself and as a way of working with the Bible.

As will be evident from chapter three, the experience of interfaith dialogue, has been very formative in my work with Bible. Perhaps I should briefly sketch the train of events that led to this. In 1964 I was involved with a Jewish youth conference in Holland. A group of young Jews from Germany pointed out that people were willing to invite them to other countries but no one came to Germany. If we were serious about the future of Jewish life in Europe, we had to come to that country. That challenge scared and impressed me at the same time and we indeed had the courage to arrange for a conference to be held in Berlin the following year, the first international Jewish youth conference in Germany since the war. To show my own commitment when the German group went home I travelled with them to Berlin, for my first adult visit to Germany, and spent a bewildering week there. On the train returning home I knew, in a moment of utter clarity, that I had made the decision somewhere within myself to become a Rabbi, something I had been vaguely considering for some years.

The contacts I made in Berlin eventually led me, together with some fellow Rabbinic students, to the Hedwig Dransfeld Haus in the little town of Bendorf, near Koblenz. It was a Catholic conference centre run by a remarkable woman, Anneliese Debray, who had dedicated the place after the war to the work of reconciliation – German-Polish, German-French – and now wanted to work in the area of German-Jewish relations. We attended a Whitsun conference and the impact of three young student Rabbis was quite extraordinary – on us no less than on the Germans, meeting for the first time Jewish young people willing to talk to them. On the spot we decided to return in the summer when the house ran a Bible study week, and thus was born the Bendorf Jewish-Christian Bible Week, that celebrated in 1990 its twenty-second year. We began with Genesis chapter one and have worked our way annually through to the beginning of Jeremiah. (I still feel guilty that we skipped Leviticus, but I did not feel qualified to teach it at the time and hope to return to it eventually!)

The point about the Bible Week was that it brought together the highly charged issues of the German-Jewish past with the even older problems of Jewish-Christian relations, and the Bible study became both a shared text that allowed us to work together and a point of departure for exploring all the other problems. The first Bible Weeks were extraordinarily painful precisely because of all the personal engagement and problems that people brought with them.

But they were also, perhaps even because of this, equally enriching. We could not afford in such circumstances to be merely polite – people brought with them very searching questions about their own lives, the problems of German, and indeed Christian, guilt in their treatment of the Jews, and a deep curiosity about the teachings and values of Judaism. Bendorf has spoiled me, in that I cannot any more cope with the superficiality of much that passes for 'dialogue'. The Bible has become inextricably bound up for me with the challenges of such a meeting between the text and people, between the struggle to understand what it says and the enormous variety of interpretations that our respective religious traditions have brought to it. But the Bible Week has never been restricted to the 'religious' approach alone. It has also given me the opportunity to invite poets, writers, artists, psychotherapists and people from a variety of other callings to share with us the insights they bring from their art, their discipline or their own personal creativity. This brings to our studies enormous richness as well as the excitement and power of personal commitment. The implications of this multifaceted approach are perhaps best summed up by Franz Rosenzweig, the great German Jewish philosopher and educationalist, the collaborator with Martin Buber. Deeply committed to 'dialogue' himself he writes that when someone comes to him with a scholarly question, he tries to answer not the scholarly question but the person who has asked it.

Which leads me to the genesis of this book and what I would like to offer with it. For many years I have been writing essays on aspects of the Bible, largely addressed to a Christian audience, some of them published in *The Month*. I was always conscious when so doing that they might make up materials for a book, if I could ever find the time. The coincidence of a long-delayed sabbatical and discussions with Dr John Bowden of SCM Press with whom I share yet another dialogue group, led to this project. But with it arose a real question. While all the individual pieces, which effectively make up the second part of this book, address separate issues, what was the book really about? What did I want to say? I assume, or hope, I have found out in the course of writing it.

I would like to offer something different to the caricatures I sketched above of much current popular Bible writing.

I came to the 'Bible' in a serious way relatively late and have had the particular pleasure of 'discovering' it for myself. Not only the Bible but also the rich traditions of interpretation, particularly

Jewish ones, that accompany it. So I want to convey something of the excitement and fun of that process of discovery, and self-discovery, but do it in a way that still leaves it open for others to make their own journey.

Secondly as a Rabbi, I have a different 'Bible' (the 'Hebrew Bible' for want of a better term, but see below) from the Christian 'Old Testament', whether in the marvellous cadences of the King James version or the more upmarket modern translations. It is, of course, in most respects the same Bible – but the different ordering of the books in the Jewish editions, the absence of a 'New Testament', and, above all, the opportunity I have to read it in the original Hebrew, all make for exciting differences of understanding and emphasis.

I also have over two thousand years of ongoing Jewish traditions of interpretation to call on that were shaped by some of the greatest minds in Jewish history. We only have to realize that in earlier centuries the sort of genius that belongs to a Freud, Einstein or Mahler would have been devoted to interpreting the Bible. What boundless creativity must have emerged from their reading. Names like Rashi, Maimonides, Abraham Ibn Ezra, Nahmanides, ought to be in the pantheon of our own collective Western culture.

But apart from the value of their own particular insights, knowing something about a living tradition of this duration and quality also gives a valuable perspective on any 'new' and 'ultimate' interpretations we discover today. On a personal level, provided I do not become awed into silence by such a tradition, it offers a firm controlling discipline to my own wilder readings. My teacher, Rav (Rabbi) Shmuel Sperber, used to get terribly anxious when he discovered a *hiddush*, a new idea or reading, and would rush to the great commentators of the past to find someone who had discovered it before. You have to have known the man to realize the delightful mixture of humour, self-deprecation and religious seriousness that underlay this need to ally himself with the tradition.

But having such a range of views available also helps us develop a useful detachment when reading what used to be called the 'assured results of modern scholarship'. All scholarship is also timebound and limited by the values and views of its era, though it is often hard to recognize that when we are living in the middle of it.

There may be a temptation at this point for those who believe that religion is above such fashions to start gloating at the limitations of 'scholarship'. However it must be pointed out that that same long

tradition of interpretation is no less challenging to the belief that we
will find in the Bible definite statements, clear answers and 'eternal
truths' – especially those that reinforce our own particular religious
position. The Bible is always in dialogue with us, believers and
non-believers alike – and what seems to matter is less the 'truth' we
discover than the integrity with which we try to struggle with that
'truth' and assimilate it into our lives.

The Rabbis summed up this view very nicely when they pointed
out that at the burning bush, God introduced himself to Moses as
the 'God of Abraham, the God of Isaac and the God of Jacob' – but
not as the 'God of Abraham, Isaac and Jacob'. Why is this the case?
Because each of the patriarchs had to discover God for himself out
of his own experience in his own time, certain only that it was the
same God. If the Rabbis are right, then this process never stops, and
the act of interpreting the Bible is our own way, in each generation,
of entering the same process of discovery, but carrying with us as we
do it, all the understandings and lessons of the past.

Somewhere within these boundaries lies the 'Bible' I would like
to share and explore – if I can find the way.

At this stage, a number of technical matters need to be addressed.

I am conscious whenever I work with the Hebrew Bible of how
little I know. For this reason I try not to cheat – that is to say to go
beyond what I do know in explaining a text. I usually do it by
becoming significantly silent at the point at which I cannot go any
further. The perceptive reader may spot such moments – others
may become a bit frustrated because their own view or question is
not addressed.

If what I do not know about the Bible is a lot, what I do not know
about Rabbinic Judaism is even greater. This is not false modesty
(as can be easily tested) nor is it particularly bad – the tradition is
indeed vast and itself seeks to inculcate a degree of caution in
speaking on its behalf. But there is one particular consequence of
this that should be noted. We who have to write sermons have got
into the bad habit of introducing significant matters with words like:
'The Rabbis say . . .' or 'Our sages have taught . . .' Now on the
whole we don't make up the statements that follow (at least most of
my colleagues don't), but we do get a bit vague about who exactly
'said' or 'taught' that particular bit of wisdom and when or where he
did it. Part of the problem lies in the fact that we have picked up a lot
of these ideas and genuinely do not know anymore where exactly we

heard or read them, and all too often we do not have the time to find out. More seriously, we sometimes confuse a particular saying in the telling, or ascribe it to the wrong Rabbi in the wrong century and the wrong movement – or even, heaven forfend, confuse it with something we heard from somewhere else entirely, but which sounds like it belongs in Rabbinic tradition.

One consequence of this vagueness, which quite rightly upsets those who value precision, is that we give the impression that Jewish tradition is monolithic – and that any old saying, which might have been very much a minority view, was the authentic expression of the totality of Jewish values. All of which is merely to say that where I can locate such remarks I will try to do so. Where I cannot, or where I find myself muddying the water by putting the right interpretation into the wrong context, I will either point this out, if I notice, or glide carefully over it.

Incidentally this concern with quoting accurately in someone's name is firmly enshrined in the Talmud. Traditions are always handed down in the name of the author, or even the person who received it from the author and in turn handed it on. It is a nice reflection of the fact that the Hebrew Bible speaks of 'history' as *toledot*, 'generations', the relationship with the past expressed in terms of continuity with remembered ancestors rather than as abstract forces.

I mention this problem of accurate transmission because I can think of at least two different sources for the interpretation I just gave about the patriarchs each finding God in their own way – but they were tied to the later use of the phrase 'God of Abraham, God of Isaac and God of Jacob' in the Jewish liturgy and not, as it appears for the first time, in Exodus 3.6. As you can imagine, giving all these possible sources might turn out to be a very complicated process, complete with massive footnotes, so let me apologize in advance to those who like precision and request that you do not write to me asking for the exact source of some anonymous saying.

I have already alluded to the problem of what to call this book, or library of books, known as the Bible. The term 'Hebrew Bible' serves to distinguish it from the 'Greek Bible', which can mean the 'New Testament', but also the Septuagint, the Greek translation of the 'Old Testament'. Difficulties arise because the words used to describe the Bible have too many polemic overtones. For Jews to hear that their 'Testament' is 'Old' and therefore in some way superseded by the 'New', is unacceptable. Nevertheless, Jews have to acknowledge that this is the case for many strands of Christianity and that there is a complex range of understandings of the relationship between the two parts of the Christian scriptures reflected in major divisions within the church itself.

But what else to call it?

There are a number of Jewish terms that serve different needs. Perhaps the most common today is the strange formulation *tenakh* (the *kh* is pronounced like the *ch* in Lo*ch* Lomond). It is an acronym made up of the first letters of the Hebrew words used to describe the three divisions of the Hebrew Bible in the Jewish canon. The 'Five Books of Moses', *Torah*; the 'Prophets', *Nevi'im*, beginning with Joshua and ending with Malachi; and the 'Writings', *Ketuvim*, from Psalms to the end of the Books of Chronicles. The three initial letters *t – n – kh* produce this neutral descriptive term which seems to have come into popular use with the revival of Hebrew in the last century.

But there are other terms in use. Perhaps the most familiar is the word 'Torah' which requires a little explanation. It is derived from a Hebrew root *yarah* which means 'to shoot arrows at a target'. It seems to mean therefore something that points the way, indicates a direction and indeed conducts you on that way. The old translations of the Bible, perhaps because of the view that the 'Old Testament' was particularly concerned with 'law', as opposed to God's 'love' or 'grace' as allegedly featured in the 'New', rendered it as 'Law', and it is indeed used sometimes to mean a particular individual 'statute' or piece of legislation. But that is to limit a word which has far broader implications, and more recent translations prefer to use a word like 'teaching', in the sense of a body of ideas that help us conduct ourselves in the world.

Within Jewish thought the term is used initially to designate the 'Five Books of Moses', also known as the *chumash*, (again *ch* as in Lo*ch*) a word derived from the Hebrew for the number five. This meaning is still retained when speaking of the three divisions of the Bible, with the latter two, the 'Prophets' and 'Writings' being seen as successive rings, like onion skins, around the central core of the Torah. But in time the term came to mean the entire Hebrew Bible, and then the traditions of interpretation (the Oral Torah) that accompany it and indeed the committed study of all these traditions and their practice. In the end Torah becomes a way of defining not only a body of knowledge but an entire way of life lived under divine guidance and providence. In a sense it is 'the Way', with both implications of the word: the path to tread and the means to reach a destination, as an individual and as part of a people.

Another term that has a different set of echoes is *miqra*, from the root *qara*, meaning 'to read' or 'call'. This derives from the idea that before 'scripture' was a 'script' that everyone could have available to them in written form, it was an oral tradition, or at least one that was regularly read aloud to the people. The same root is used in the first word of the Book of Leviticus, 'He (God) *called* to Moses', so it contains the sense as well of personal revelation, of 'calling'. It is familiar to us indirectly because of the 'Koran', the sacred book of Islam, derived from a similar Arabic root. *'miqra'* is therefore a particularly religious term for the 'Bible' as divine revelation and is firmly anchored in Rabbinic tradition.

In what follows I will usually employ the term 'Bible' to designate the 'Hebrew Bible', unless this leads to confusion in a particular instance.

There is a second problem of designations that has acquired a new nuance today as a result of the search for 'inclusive language'. The anger that discussion of this matter evokes merely reinforces the view that it is very important. I personally find it a significant issue and will try to be sensitive to it in general in writing this book. The particular problem that arises in connection with the Bible has to do with the use of words for God. The first of the two most prominent ones in the Bible is *elohim* which seems to be a generic term designating not only Israel's God, but also God as known to other peoples, 'gods', and even idols (the phrase 'other gods'), or even figures in the divine assembly, plus some secular terms like 'judge'. The term 'God' is helpfully 'non-gender specific' for this purpose – though the story is told about a little boy who insisted that God was masculine. 'Why' asked his mother? 'Because "God" sounds like a boy's name!' came the irresistible reply.

Difficulties arise with the other major name, the tetragrammaton, the four letter name of God which became the particular and exclusive name for Israel's deity. (A very gifted Israeli girl I once knew, Miri Farber, alas killed long ago in a car accident, told me that she used to think of *elohim* as God's surname, and the other as God's personal one.) It is spelled with the Hebrew letters *yod – hey – vav – hey*, and would seem to be related to the hebrew verb meaning 'to be'. But how do you pronounce it? There is already a tradition, recorded from the time of the second Temple, that one should not even attempt to pronounce it – that was restricted to the

High Priest and then only on the holiest day of the year, the Day of Atonement, in the Temple as part of the ritual of the day. It was uttered even then at great personal risk to the High Priest. So there arose a tradition of substituting instead *adonay*, a word meaning 'lord', which often occurs in the Bible in situations where it would appear to be interchangeable with the tetragrammaton.

But it all gets complicated at this point. Some traditional Jews felt it inappropriate even to pronounce this substituted name, and found alternatives – for example when practising the recital of the Bible for the ritual reading in Synagogue, or learning the blessing formula. So various alternatives are available, most commonly perhaps *hashem*, which simply means 'the name'. There is a well known consequence for Christianity of this substitution. In order to indicate in the Hebrew text that we do not attempt to pronounce the tetragrammaton, when it is written out, the vowels of the substitute word *adonay* are added to the consonants Y – H – V – H. Christians, unaware of this, assumed the vowels belonged to this particular set of letters and tried to pronounce it. The result is something like *'yehovah*, hence indeed the name 'Jehovah', which is a curious concoction and thoroughly illegitimate as a term.

More recent translations have indeed attempted to pronounce the 'name' and have come up with 'Yahweh'. Apart from being offensive to traditional Jewish sensitivities, the disadvantage is that it makes the name into a sort of 'proper name' – like Milcom or Baal or Dagan, other contemporary Near Eastern gods. Yet the essence of this name seems to lie in its not being the designated name of a god like any other. It is less a proper name than a hint at some essence or qualities.

But having said all that, how do you translate the name? One common tradition has been to accept the relationship with the word *adonay* and translate it as 'Lord', though this is still the translation of a substitute word. Another attempt may be traced back in Germany to the Bible translation of the Jewish philosopher Moses Mendelssohn (1729–86), who understood the verb 'to be' to indicate a sense of 'timelessness', 'eternity'. Hence he translated the name as 'der Ewige', 'the Eternal'.

In this century, Martin Buber and Franz Rosenzweig, struggling with the same problem in their own translation of the Bible into German tried something entirely different. They saw in the root 'to be' not just God's 'eternity', but continual 'being', 'being with' and indeed 'presence'. So they wrote instead of God as 'He who is' and

in their actual translation into German did not translate the
tetragrammaton at all but inserted instead the pronouns 'HE',
'YOU' or 'I' in capital letters as appropriate to the context.
My Bible teacher at Leo Baeck College, Dr Ellen Littmann,
pointed out that these two options were reflected in a significant way
in the writings of Rabbi Dr Leo Baeck. Baeck who was the spiritual
leader of German Jewry in the period before and during the Nazi
period wrote a book earlier in the century called *The Essence of
Judaism*. It was a serious examination of the principles of Judaism
that still stands up today. In it he used the word 'Eternal' when
translating the name of God. Baeck left Germany in 1939 with a
group of Jewish refugee children, but refused the offer of a haven
abroad and returned instead to be with his community in Germany.
The war found him in Berlin where he continued teaching Midrash
and Jewish Thought at the great liberal Rabbinic seminary, the
Hochschule fuer die Wissenschaft des Judentums (College for the
Scientific Study of Judaism) until the Nazis closed it in 1942. (They
had kept it open as a way of showing the outside world how well they
treated their Jewish citizens.) Baeck was taken to Theresienstadt, a
'model' concentration camp, again for outside consumption. There
he continued to give lectures on the history of culture and
civilization, as if to assert the retention of human values despite the
dehumanization of the Nazi period. He was put on a death list but
survived because another Rabbi with a similar name was taken by
mistake instead. Baeck survived the war, incidentally preventing
his fellow prisoners turning on their guards when they were
liberated. He spent the rest of his life commuting between the
United Kingdom and America where he taught at the Hebrew
Union College in Cincinatti. In Theresienstadt he worked on his
second great book, *This People Israel*. Dr Littmann pointed out that
in this book, perhaps precisely because of the need to assert the
presence of God in such suffering, Baeck uses the more intimate
formula, 'He who is'. Instead of the 'Eternal', the 'God of the
philosophers', he had turned to the One who is there, to be met in
personal encounter.

Unfortunately the device that Buber and Rosenzweig use is
clumsy and, because they had to use 'HE', becomes difficult today,
as does the term 'Lord', precisely because such terms, consciously
or unconsciously, assert the 'masculinity' of God. However much
we insist that this idea as theologically unacceptable, and that we do
not think that God has a particular gender, nevertheless the

repeated use of the language does actually influence us and affect our societies and religions. In essence we give a warrant to the perpetuation of hierarchies in which power and authority lie with males. For all these reasons I have settled for using the terms 'God' or 'the Eternal' as appropriate to the translation or context, though I acknowledge the inadequacy of the latter.

If I have one image that helps me understand what I might be trying to achieve with this book, it is one I learned from another Bible enthusiast who had a powerful effect on me when I first began my Rabbinic journey. I met Pastor Rudolph Stamm in Dusseldorf. He was visiting a friend, another Pastor, I had come to know through a circle of left-wing Pastors in Germany. Rudolph was still in the middle of his final exams when we met, but, in one of those strange encounters that are so utterly surprising, we found ourselves enormously caught up with each other, and repaired to a Stube to drink wine and exchange poetry, in his extravagant English and my pidgin German. He had grown up in Nazi Germany and it was only the encounter with an English equivalent of the National Socialist mentality after the war that gave him a perspective on what had happened to him. When I first heard his story I began to understand how simple it was to become caught up in that whole Nazi madness, and to wonder whether I would have been able to see through it, if my Jewishness would not have condemned me to be its victim.

But Rudolph had a particular vision that caught my imagination. He wanted to have a building with a large show window overlooking the street. People passing by would see that the room inside was filled with people seemingly very happy with what they were doing. Curious they would enter to ask what was going on here, to learn that the people were studying Bible together. For that vision and much else Rudolph was another impetus to my concern with Bible and more specifically the Bendorf Bible week which is the nearest thing I know to his picture window.

Enough explanations. Let us enter the world of the Bible through the route commonly open to us, whatever our language, through 'reading' – and learn something of how difficult an art it actually is.

2

Learning How to Read

At one of the Soviet party congresses, so the story goes, Stalin held up a telegram which he said he had just received from the disgraced Trotsky. 'This is what he now confesses!' said the dictator triumphantly, and read:

I WAS WRONG – STOP – YOU WERE RIGHT – STOP – YOU SHOULD BE LEADER – STOP.

This was greeted with three minutes of thunderous applause. But as Stalin was about to sit down, a hand went up in the middle of the hall and a little old man stood up. 'Pardon me, comrade Stalin,' came a hesitant voice, 'but I think you may have read the telegram incorrectly.' Silence fell. Stalin said nothing and waited. 'What comrade Trotsky actually meant to say (and here, gentle reader, I fear you must provide your own emphasis in what follows) is:

I WAS *WRONG*?! – STOP – YOU WERE RIGHT?! – STOP – *YOU* SHOULD BE LEADER?!?

This story is particularly revealing because it mimics one of the fundamental problems about reading the Hebrew Bible – namely that the text itself is utterly lacking in what we would think of as punctuation. It is true that there is a long tradition of how to read individual words and sentences, and indeed how to break up the sentences into smaller sub-units. All these are found in the 'Masoretic text', the version of the Hebrew Bible preserved in Jewish tradition. But these traditional punctuation marks are relatively late in the written form in which we have them – about the seventh century of the current era. Moreover they do not correspond in any way to the question marks, exclamation marks, quotation signs or other symbols that we rely on in Western languages to give us a sense of how the sentence is broken up. They tell us how to divide the sentence into smaller sense units but little more than that. Incidentally these same signs that serve to break up the sentences are actually indications of musical notes that allow the passage to be chanted in the synagogue.

You may remember an old classroom test in English language. What punctuation marks do you have to add to this sentence so as to make sense of it? 'John where James had had had had had had had had had had had a better effect on the teacher.' For those who want to have a go at punctuating it yourself, without cheating, I will save the answer, or at least 'an answer' till the end of this chapter.

Now while the Masoretic punctuation is very helpful in determining how a sentence is to be broken up, and is usually a matter of common sense, nevertheless there is evidence of disagreements within that tradition about many cases. Furthermore, for the purposes of interpreting the text, the Rabbis were prepared to treat it in a seemingly cavalier way, taking out bits and pieces apparently at random to suit their own purposes. The reasons for this freedom have to be understood. For them the Hebrew Bible in its entirety was the word of God, so every sentence, word, even letter, was full of meaning which could be legitimately extracted and interpreted entirely by itself, given the right spirit of enquiry and intention.

Despite the existence of this tradition, it is nevertheless perfectly legitimate to ignore it entirely and go behind it to the unvocalized text such as you would see still today in the Scrolls of the Torah that are read in Synagogue. These contain a text in which the words are made up of the consonants alone with no guidelines at all as to how they are to be pronounced – apart from one's own knowledge or experience of the language. *Y gt th sns f hw dffclt t s f y tk t th vwls frm sntnc nd tr t rd t.* Depending on your understanding of the above sentence, or your particular orientation, you may read the fourth word as 'sense', 'sins', 'sons' or any other variant. Fortunately reading the 'unpointed' Hebrew text is not quite as hard as all that, but it is important to realize that we are dealing with a text we cannot in any way take for granted. In most cases the word itself, or the word in a particular context, make the general sense quite clear, but there are many occasions where it is not at all evident what is actually going on. Those who only work with English or other translations do not realize this because the translator has made a decision for us about the sense of the sentence as a whole, but it only needs a brief comparison of a few translations to see how varied they can be about certain passages.

When addressing audiences that do not have access to Hebrew I
tend to overplay its importance. Obviously the general outlines of a
story can be followed and much of the poetry remains, at least as a
new creation which echoes the original. But the Hebrew of the
Bible is a language with a relatively limited vocabulary, thus there is
an enormous amount of hidden interaction between words that
serve a variety of different meanings. These interconnections are
often lost in the translation and a whole dimension of meaning with
them. Moreover it has a particular style of syntax and structure
which also comes into play in the conveying of ideas, of emphasis, of
nuance – unless one creates a hebraized English (which in many
ways the King James Bible is) that whole dimension is missing.
Apart from that the sounds, rhythms, the 'music', is also sacrificed
and these dimensions also make an enormous difference to the
'taste', 'feeling', inner coherence and integrity of the text itself. The
Psalmist says in the RSV version:

> Pray for the peace of Jerusalem!
> May they prosper who love you!
> Peace be within your walls
> and security within your towers! (Ps. 122.6–7)

The alliteration of the 'p's' (pray . . . peace . . . prosper) is a brave
attempt to capture something of the intent of the original. But listen
for a moment to the Hebrew in which there is a continuous word
play on the name of Jerusalem (*yerushalayim*), the word for 'peace'
(*shalom*), for ask/'pray for' (*sha'alu*) and to be quiet, at ease
('prosper' and 'security' in the RSV) (*yishlayu* and *shalvah*):

> *sha'alu sh'lom yerushalayim*
> *yishlayu ohavayikh*
> *yehi shalom b'heilakh*
> *shalvah b'arm'notayikh*

The repeated use of the letter *shin* and the soft lingual *lamed*, as well
as the quiet rhythm, convey precisely that sense of peace and ease
that the Psalmist seeks. The name of Jerusalem, the state of peace it
should reach, even the sounds that express that wish, all blend into
an extraordinary unity. It can be translated but not transmitted.

To return to the Trotsky story, there is a nice example of how the
Rabbis could also read, or misread, a text. With this we also enter
the difficult area of deciding when an interpretation is legitimately
what the text intends (exegesis, 'reading out') and when it is a

'reading in' of our own values (eisegesis). Though it can be argued that all interpretation is a sort of 'reading in' however objective we think we are being (see the discussion at the end of the next chapter).

When Jacob, egged on by his mother, pretended to be his brother Esau so as to steal his firstborn blessing, he had to identify himself to his father.

There are a number of ways of looking at the story as a whole. Those who come to it with no preconceived ideas can be forgiven for thinking of Jacob as a thief and indeed a pretty obnoxious character at that in taking advantage of his father's blindness. Those who come with a more traditional sense of the worth of Jacob, as the founder of the Jewish people, try to seek ways of explaining or justifying his behaviour. He was, after all, acting under the orders of his mother, herself motivated by a prophetic revelation she received when the two children were still in her womb (Gen. 25.22–24).

A middle way is to recognize that whereas we are prone to identify with the hero of a story and take for granted the legitimacy of his or her actions, we can also identify with the position of the anonymous writer and look for evidence of his or her views about what is going on. When subsequently Jacob's father-in-law Laban switches brides with him on his wedding night, so that Jacob is misled into marrying Leah the older sister in place of his beloved Rachel, the younger one, Laban's self-justification exactly echoes and thus repays Jacob for what he did: 'That's not the way we do things here, to give the younger one in place of the firstborn!' (Gen. 28.26). There are other echoes throughout the story to suggest that Jacob never escapes from what he did (betrayals continue to haunt him through the lives of his own children). So in a way we are able to see Jacob as a flawed character who nevertheless develops through his life.

But what of the event itself? Did Jacob participate willingly or unwillingly, out of the desire for personal aggrandisement or simple obedience to his mother's wishes? The question remains open, but for one mediaeval Jewish commentator in particular there was clearly a need to justify Jacob's behaviour, and he found in the text a peg with which to get Jacob off the hook, to mix a couple of metaphors.

When Isaac asks the identity of the son who had appeared with his favourite food, Jacob has to answer (Gen. 27.18–19).

He came to his father and said: 'My father.' He said: 'Here I am. Who are you, my son?' Jacob said to his father: 'Esau, your firstborn. I did what you told me. Please rise up, sit and eat my game so that your soul can bless me.'

From the discussion that follows it is not at all clear whether Isaac is actually taken in by Jacob or not, which adds a further dimension of difficulty to understanding the story. But at the precise point where Jacob states that he is Esau, Rashi, the great mediaeval Jewish Bible commentator whom we shall meet properly later, introduces his own surprising bit of punctuation. The three hebrew words are *'anokhi esav bekhorekha'*, literally 'I – Esau – your firstborn'. The word for 'I' is one of two words used for this pronoun, the other being *'ani'*. The form used here, *'anokhi'*, is used by God at the very beginning of the Ten Commandments, perhaps for its emphatic effect, 'I (*anokhi*) am the Eternal your God who brought you out from the land of Egypt.' What is interesting with regards Jacob is that a few verses later on, when he must once again admit to the false identity (verse 24), he uses the other word for 'I':

He said: 'Are you really my son Esau?' He said: *'ani*, I (am).'

It may be that the use of these two different forms of the word for 'I' within the same context made Rashi ponder the difference between them and gave him the justification for doing a radical re-writing of the sentence – or rather, to take advantage of the lack of punctuation so as to break up the sentence and make it work in a totally different way, even contradicting the traditional reading of the Masoretic text. He has Jacob saying:

anokhi I am the one who brings [food] to you. *esav bekhorekha* and Esau is your firstborn!

Presumably Rashi would have argued that the word *'anokhi'* is so special and even emphatic that Jacob, under great stress and distress, tried to make clear who he really was so that his father could find out and take some responsibility for what followed. On the level of possible readings, it is justifiable. On the lines of the apparent thrust of the text, let alone the traditional sentence divisions, it would seem quite untenable. Moreover, it is a highly dubious way of justifying Jacob's unjustifiable behaviour. So we are forced into a second level of interpretation, namely trying to discover what led Rashi, who was clearly aware of the problem of what he was doing, nevertheless to go for such a reading 'against the text'. I cannot offer any direct answer, beyond the general situation of Rashi in the context of the Christian world of his time and the constant religious pressures on the Jewish community. Jacob symbolized Israel, so every detail of his behaviour would be open to scrutiny as a way of attacking the community. Perhaps in such a context Rashi had to find a way of justifying Jacob as a form of self-defence and apologetics.

My point, however is not Rashi's interpretation, but the way in which the text is open to precisely such reading and re-reading because of its very nature and the lack of punctuation. While this comes from a story and it is possible to give some measure of control over how it should be read, there are many passages where it is far more difficult to decide what precisely the emphasis should be. One famous verse in particular can be read in two totally opposite ways, in exactly the same manner as the Trotsky telegram.

Isaiah chapter one contains a magnificent polemic against hypocrisy in religious practice, particularly where it is aligned with acts of injustice. At a climactic point the prophet challenges his hearers to stand in court together with God and themselves judge the situation (Isa. 1.18).

> Come, let us reason together, says the Eternal.
> If your sins are as crimson,
> they shall be as white as snow;
> if they are red as scarlet,
> they shall become like wool!

God seems to hold out here a promise of endless forgiveness, an idea that will have a long theological development. But . . . without the least change of the Masoretic text, or even any unusual interpretation, the entire passage could be read instead as sarcastic and scornful, that is to say, the opposite of the above and a direct continuation of the mood and mode of the powerful polemic that precedes it.

> Come let us reason together, says the Eternal.
> If your sins are as crimson,
> shall they be as white as snow?!
> if they are red as scarlet
> shall they become like wool?!

Examples of this sort could be multiplied endlessly. We are entering here into the very heart of the problem of reading a text and of our expectations when we do so. Is there only one reading, one meaning possible, or is it the measure of a text as rich and challenging as the Bible that it is constantly open to re-reading? Must we be confined to what a particular tradition or authority defines as the 'authentic' meaning or should we be free to acknowledge a variety of possibilities? Where do you draw the line on this freedom? Traditionalists have always tried to fix the meaning to justify the status quo; reformers have always appealed to the Bible to offer an alternative.

It is clearly absurd, let alone intellectually dishonest, to deny the possibilities of multiple readings. Nevertheless we all make our own private or collective rules, set our own boundaries, so that we can say what is 'true' or at least 'acceptable' for our own selves or our community. In the next chapter we will look at a variety of different individual approaches to the text, partly because they are interesting in themselves, partly because they remind us that the Bible is not anyone's exclusive property, nor is its interpretation.

In making the above remarks I am deeply influenced by Jewish tradition. To put it at its simplest, monotheism introduces into the world a God who is both present and totally other, invisible and yet active in history, unknowable yet available to our experience. The paradoxes can be multiplied, but they leave the faith community with the problem of an invisible, immaterial God who must nevertheless be acknowledged by visible and material human beings. That is to say for us even to begin to relate to such a God, individually and collectively, we have to establish some point of contact and relationship.

The biblical idea of the covenant gave the Jewish people a particular frame of reference that determined above all their conduct, in terms of their interrelationships with each other and those outsiders resident amongst them, their responsibilities to the land itself, their duties to God. It was these 'conditions of the contract', perceived in a limited way as 'law', that become one great pole of the Jewish exposition of the Bible. As Rav Sperber once put it, but probably more gracefully, what kind of a God would He be to put us in charge of the world without giving us some idea of how to run it?

So one task in working with Bible, and all the subsequent classical Jewish texts, was to define and refine and constantly update the rules of conduct for an entire civilization. What this meant was that collective decisions were made about practice, everything from the

conduct of law courts to behaviour in the bedroom, from building
regulations and town planning to food preparation. In these
concrete areas of behaviour the Jewish people found their own way
of anchoring, fixing, securing the will and intention of God as
expressed through the traditions of revelation and the accepted
modes of interpretation.

But, and it is an enormous 'but', whereas practice was regulated,
thoughts, imagination, creativity, were to remain unbounded.
Security lay in the practice, and that freed the mind to explore
wherever it wished. The Rabbinic saying 'There are seventy faces to
Torah' epitomizes this openness. As does the enormous breadth of
discussion and the richness of different interpretation throughout
Rabbinic literature, including the careful recording of all minority
views in legal decisions, so that discussions could always be
reopened.

To give a sense of this I need only quote a well-known piece by
Abraham Joshua Heschel, a product both of the rich, hasidic
culture of Eastern Europe and the rigorous academic world of pre-
war Western European scholarship. He speaks here of two terms,
two poles of Jewish religious life, *halakhah*, Jewish 'law', though
the word means literally 'walking', perhaps 'conduct', and *aggadah*,
literally 'narrating', which contains all the richness of Jewish
imaginative openness to the world.

Halakhah represents the strength to shape one's life according to
a fixed pattern; it is a form-giving force. *Aggadah* is the
expression of man's ceaseless striving, which often defies all
limitations. *Halakhah* is the rationalization and schematization of
living; it defines, specifies, sets measure and limit, placing life into
an exact system. *Aggadah* deals with man's ineffable relations to
God, to other men, and to the world. *Halakhah* deals with
details, with each commandment separately; *aggadah* with the
whole of life, with the totality of religious life. *Halakhah* deals
with the law, *aggadah* with the meaning of the law. *Halakhah*
deals with subjects that can be expressed literally; *aggadah*
introduces us to a realm which lies beyond the range of
expression. *Halakhah* teaches us how to perform common acts;
aggadah tells us how to participate in the eternal drama.
Halakhah gives us knowledge; *aggadah* exaltation. *Halakhah*
prescribes, *aggadah* suggests; *halakhah* decrees, *aggadah* in-
spires; *halakhah* is definite, *aggadah* is allusive.

To maintain that the essence of Judaism consists exlcusively of *halakhah* is as erroneous as to maintain that the essence of Judaism consists exclusively of *aggadah*. The interrelationship of *halakhah* and *aggadah* is the very heart of Judaism. *Halakhah* without *aggadah* is dead, *aggadah* without *halakhah* is wild.

These same parameters were beautifully summed up by another traditional Rabbi I have had the privilege of studying with from time to time, Dr E. Wiesenberg.

A *baal halakhah* (a master of *halakhah*, but *halakhah* alone) is a naked giant; a *baal aggadah* (a master of the aggadic tradition alone) is a dwarf in full panoply!

My suspicion is that the converse of this kind of approach, one that fixes practice yet leaves the mind free, is that which, at least from the outside, seems to be the choice of Christianity. It is in dogma, in right belief, that the community is defined and determined, that security is gained. And right belief implies wrong belief and heresy, and ultimately considerable restrictions on the breadth of freedom and creativity. I recognize that there may be here something of a caricature, and that there are many 'christianitys' (perhaps as a result), but all monotheistic faiths have to cope with the tendency that monotheism becomes monolatry, that one God alone comes to assume one kind of believer alone. In such a context the multiple dimensions of the Hebrew Bible become not merely interesting, or disturbing, they provide the key for endless self-critique and renewal. They are not inconvenient complications to our finding the 'truth', they are of the very essence of that 'truth' – our task is to find strategies for living with this plurality. Or as Rav Sperber once put it:

Religion offers answers without obliterating the questions. They become blunted and will not attack you with the same ferocity. But without them the answer would dry up and wither away. The question is a great religious act; it helps you live great religious truth.

I want to close this chapter with a particular story that was very influential in my understanding of how to read Bible. But first there are two little details that have to be tidied up.

I said earlier that the Masoretic tradition did not offer equivalents to question marks and other ways of punctuating with which we are familiar. There is one delightful exception to this, a mark, which is also a note for chanting, called the *shalshelet*. The word means 'chain', is drawn to look like a coiled spring and is chanted with a long quavering note. It can be found in only three places in the Book of Genesis, and each time indicates some degree of uncertainty on the part of the subject of the story. The first time is when Lot is instructed by his angelic visitors to leave Sodom before it is destroyed. Despite the frightening treatment he has just had at the hands of the townspeople, Lot is unwilling to go, perhaps because of his material investment in the area. At the crucial moment of decision he hesitated (Gen. 19.16) and above the word for 'hesitate' comes the *shalshelet* to reinforce the sense of his dithering.

The second occurrence comes when Abraham sends his servant back to his birthplace to find a wife for Isaac. The servant stands by the well and sets out a kind of condition for God so as to fulfil the task. The Rabbis evidently saw in this testing of God something that made the servant a bit nervous, and over the word 'He said', which introduces his request (Gen. 24.12) comes again the *shalshelet*.

But the third case is the most dramatic. Joseph is tempted by the wife of Potiphar to sleep with her. In the sentence that follows, we can hear Joseph desperately weighing up the arguments – and indeed the more he brings, the more hard he is fighting against the temptation to accept. 'Methinks the lady (or gentleman) doth protest too much!'

But he refused and said to the wife of his master: 'Look, even my master does not know as much as I do about what is in the household and he has put everything he has into my care. No one is greater in this household than I am and he has withheld from me nothing except you since you are his wife, so how could I do such a great evil thing, and moreover sin against God!' (Gen. 39.8–9)

Joseph convinces himself but it was a close call. The Rabbis recognized just how close, and above the apparently forthright opening word 'But he refused!' they placed the third *shalshelet*.

The other piece of unfinished business is the sentence that had to be punctuated. The version I know runs as follows:

John, where James had had 'had' had had 'had had'. 'Had had' had had a better effect on the teacher.

In 1968 our progressive Jewish youth movement hosted a group of young Czech Jews for a conference near Edinburgh. They stayed on for an additional week – and the Russians marched into Prague, cutting them off from their country and their families. Many of them became refugees overnight. That would be enough to bring them to mind, especially in the radical changes now happening in Eastern Europe, but they taught me something very special about the Bible in the time we were together. We studied some Bible texts and they were incredibly good at understanding them, picking up all the nuances very quickly. I was surprised as they had never studied the Bible before.

'It's easy,' they explained. 'You see, in Czechoslovakia, when you read a newspaper, first you read what is written there. Then you say to yourself, "If that is what they have written, what really happened? And if that is what really happened, what are they trying to make us think? And if that is what they are trying to make us think, what should we be thinking instead?" You learn to read between the lines and behind the lines. You learn to read a newspaper as if your life depended upon understanding it – because it does!'

'You learn to read a newspaper as if your life depended upon understanding it.' Sometimes the same applies to the Bible, sometimes we just have to learn how to read.

In the next chapter we will meet nine friends of mine, each in their own quite different way, readers of the Bible.

3

Nine Faces of Torah

The Rabbis spoke of 'seventy faces of Torah', by which they meant that it was open to an infinite number of interpretations. I hope we will experience something of this in the course of the book, but in this chapter I want to view this idea in a slightly different way, not in terms of interpretations but of interpreters. We will meet a variety of people, friends and colleagues of mine, who each brings his or her unique experience and commitment to the Bible. Each of them is a 'face of the Torah'.

One pragmatic reason for doing this is that the material for this chapter became available while I was working on the book, and it seemed to fit. On a deeper level I am beginning to discover as I work on it that one of my concerns is to show how wide a variety of approaches to and experiences of Bible are available and legitimate, and indeed how enriching it is to learn from and enjoy all of them. Each person brings to it their own unique personality, knowledge and life experience, each is a resource for all of us. At Sinai, said the Rabbis, everyone understood the revelation according to their own personal ability.

This plurality of readings and sharing of traditions and teachers is perhaps one of the most valuable gifts to have come from the current concern with 'dialogue', and particularly that between religions. The discussion recorded in this chapter could only have taken place because of several years investment in such work at the Jewish–Christian Bible Week in Bendorf.

Before meeting the participants, a word about dialogue from a biblical point of view may be of use. It is not something that springs to mind when contemplating the Hebrew Bible, because one's impression of the relations between biblical Israel and the other nations in the area is one of enmity, war, religious intolerance and even persecution. All of which is true, but it is surely no accident that the Torah records at least two major 'interfaith' dialogues and accords the protagonists in both cases considerable respect, largely because they treat each other and the other's knowledge of God with great respect.

When Abraham meets Melchizedek, King of Shalem (Gen. 14.18–23), it feels a bit like what must happen when the Chief Rabbi has tea with the Archbishop of Canterbury, if that is not an irrelevant (or for that matter irreverent) comparison. Both parties act with great solemnity and dignity, there is much bestowing of blessings, but all of this with just a hint of theological tension and caution. One wonders what they actually talked about when the cameras were switched off.

Abraham has just been involved in a major international military crisis and has saved his nephew Lot after a running battle. Two personages come out to meet him on his return, seemingly to pay him a percentage fee for his part in recovering the booty lost in the war: the unnamed King of the notorious town of Sodom and Melchizedek, the Priest/King of Shalem, Jerusalem in another incarnation.

> And Melchizedek King of Shalem brought out bread and wine, he being the Priest to El Elyon (the Most High God). He blessed him and said, 'Blessed be Abram to El Elyon, possessor of heaven and earth, and blessed be El Elyon who delivered your enemies into your hand'. Then he gave him a tenth of everything.
>
> Then the King of Sodom said to Abram, 'Give me the people, and keep the booty for yourself'. But Abram replied to the King of Sodom, 'I have raised my hand (in an oath) to the Eternal, El Elyon, possessor of heaven and earth, saying that neither a thread nor a shoelace nor anything that is yours shall I take so that you would be able to say, "It was I that made Abram rich!"'

Clearly a lot is going on here under the surface in terms of the present and future relations of Abraham and both personages. The contempt for the King of Sodom is clear, but nowhere directly explained. Scholars have been rightly concerned with the complex prehistory of this entire chapter. But here I only want to draw attention to the subtle way in which Abraham both accepts and honours the knowledge of God expressed by Melchizedek, but also appends the name of the Eternal to the title El Elyon when he uses the divine names. On one level this seems to reflect a remarkable assimilation of different names of God within the biblical 'family' and may reflect centuries of coming to terms with other religious traditions. Truth has to be accepted wherever it may be found. But it also has about it the air of cautious diplomacy, a sounding out of *bona fides*, perhaps quite literally in this case, clarifying what is the same and wherein lie at least some subtle differences. In short precisely the sort of niceties that occur when distinguished clerics of different religions or churches get together. (I do not want to sound unduly flippant about such an important encounter, but I have been involved in 'professional dialogue' for many years and it works on a variety of levels.)

The other 'interfaith meeting' is that between Moses and his father-in-law Jethro which appears in many strands of biblical tradition. From an 'interfaith' point of view, the whole thing is complicated somewhat by Moses' marriage to Jethro's daughter (something that makes both sides in dialogue today a little uneasy). The possibility of interfaith 'dialogue' here in the conventional sense was also somewhat challenged by the scholarly view that held sway for a long time, the Kenite hypothesis, that it was from Jethro that Moses actually learned about monotheism. Thus we would be seeing here not 'dialogue' but 'conversion'. But the hypothesis is no longer held, and nothing of that sort emerges from the discussions between Jethro and Moses. Rather what is again clear is that it is possible for the Bible to countenance other nations having a direct relationship with God (including even enemies of Israel like Balaam (Num. 22–24)). Moreover, Israel is acknowledged as owing its system of judges and courts to the intervention of Jethro, (Ex. 18) in a chapter that immediately precedes the giving of the covenant on Mount Sinai, so that the two events are inextricably intertwined.

All of which is to suggest that those engaged in religious dialogue can find precedents, of sorts, in the Bible and that the rich benefits to be gained from it are long since acknowledged. (Other biblical episodes, particularly the stories of Elijah and of Solomon (see chapter 7 for the latter) suggest a somewhat different view of the dangers of such encounters.)

This leads us conveniently into the conversations that follow that were recorded at a remarkable 'colloquium' organized for the magazine European Judaism at the Twenty-second Annual Jewish-Christian Bible Week in Bendorf. I have already spoken about the Bible Week, suffice it to say that in that particular year we had with us a remarkably rich array of biblical 'resource people' (a title less daunting than 'expert' and one that discourages them talking too much in the group work). Ten of us sat down for an hour and a half and talked about why we were so drawn to the Bible. What was exciting was the enthusiasm that came from people whom I thought regarded their work with Bible with a certain degree of academic detachment. Moreover each had a range of personal stories and emphases that evoked echoes and contrasts from the others. This chapter includes an edited version of the contributions of the other nine participants, excluding my own which is expressed more fully in this book.

I started off the discussion with a short history of my own involvement with the Bible and invited the next speaker. In what follows they tend to introduce themselves through their own remarks.

Eveline Goodman-Thau   I live in Jerusalem and the kind of things you have been saying sounded very familiar so I thought I would plug into that and tell my part of it. I was born in Vienna, my parents come from Galicia, and my father from the same town as Manes Sperber [the psychoanalyst and writer, not to be confused with my 'Rav Sperber'! JM]. One of the interesting things is that through the books of Manes Sperber I discovered what Sablotov, this little village, was all about. It was a very cosmopolitan place. People thought they were ruling the world, discussing all the important issues of their lives and of the world, and full of politics and everything. But what I actually received from my father, who came from a very hasidic background, is that the answer for the question of that week you will surely find in the portion [of the Bible read in Synagogue] of that week. It didn't matter what the topic was, but this was the important thing, in that portion you found the actual answer. So I must say that *Tenakh* was in the background always there.

Till I got there it was a very long road. I survived the war in Holland, studied English literature came then to Jerusalem to the Hebrew University to study Jewish thought. The approach was very historical-critical, so I didn't particularly enjoy it, but didn't lose my love for the text and decided after a couple of years of studying . . . to pick a text with which I would be able to do the same thing my father was doing with the portion of the week: find the answers to the questions. And so I picked . . . the *siddur* [the prayerbook] . . . eighty percent of which is *tenakh*.

So I would explain my connection to *tenakh* now on three levels. First of all, a very basic text, a kind of spiritual canon; on a very personal level and on a traditional level. This expresses something which has . . . a meaning for me . . . in its very totality, and it also connects me to the way this text has been used through the ages, by Rabbis, by people who are close to me and so on. So I am standing in a certain tradition.

An additional reason why this text is important for me is that I am a woman. I come from an orthodox background – I say I am a very unorthodox, orthodox woman – but that means that as a woman I basically am not allowed to have, in orthodoxy, a real stake in this text. The text is explained for me and things are sort of mapped out. For me, going back to the text is finding my identity as a woman in the tradition . . .

It doesn't happen to me when I read a Midrash; it doesn't happen to me when I read a Kabbalistic text; it doesn't happen through the Talmud – it happens through this text, that every time I read it, it is different. So this is the second level . . . me as the Jewish woman with this text.

And in Jewish-Christian dialogue, which I am doing for the last couple of years . . . I also found that reading with Christians opens tremendously new dimensions . . .

Philip Davies   I want to say something about the Bible as religious literature. I suppose my own career can be divided into two parts. I first of all studied the Bible as a historian, probably because I believed that its meaning lay essentially outside itself and was referring to things that could be talked about independently of the Bible. That includes, of course, God. But the history as well, the exilic background of certain songs, and so on.

I work in a department [Sheffield University] that is not in a faculty of theology but stands on its own as biblical studies. Recently I've begun to rethink what kind of discipline this is; how should one be academically studying? What is it that I am really studying? Recently I have come to accept that I am really studying the Bible itself and that its meaning resides inside it and not outside. It does not refer to something else by means of which it is validated, it is to some extent a closed universe, except that it is a rather big one. I have also come to accept that because it does not have, I think, referential meanings any more pointing to objective things outside itself its truth value does not lie in dogmatic claims. In other words it does not subscribe itself, in my opinion, to the view that there is a right meaning to derive and there is a wrong one. The religious definition of truth is, of course, that if I'm right then everyone else must be wrong. This currently arises in nearly all religion and it's difficult to know of a religion that could work in any other way. But I am increasingly interested in redeeming the Bible from religious systems. The Bible is defined as a religious document because of its use, not because of its essence.

Many of the things that the Bible talks about are things that in our own day would be called 'science'. For example, it says that God created the world. Is that a scientific statement or is it a religious one? In the ancient world everyone thought that the world was created by divine beings because they really couldn't think of anything else and our modern scientific explanations would be strange to them. They believed that gods brought diseases and gods could cure diseases. We don't believe that any more. Is it a religious belief to say that the universe is only explicable on a deistic theory – fine! If so, of course, the Bible is religious, but then so is nearly all ancient literature. I don't find myself that I can read the Bible as a 'religious document' in the modern definition, because that isn't the way in which I think the content of the Bible is religious. I find it is a remarkable, self-deconstructing, perpetually liberating and illuminating book in which the challenge is always to find out what it means and then find out immediately that it is contradicting itself, and asking you another set of questions. In other words, you come to the Bible with answers and it gives you back a question. That's what I find in the Bible so fascinating. And whether I made the right decision in getting into it I am a biblical scholar. It's made me what I am. We are kind of married together or stuck together and I am going to find in it whatever I am ever going to find and it is a perpetually challenging experience. I am only sad that I am never going to be able to live long enough to really get to grips with it.

Gordian Marshall I grew up in a fairly traditional Catholic family on the east coast of Scotland and I grew up with the idea that the Bible was something important in life and in religion but it was something which was pretty inaccessible. Because although there was always a Bible in the house, all we got in school and in religious instruction was Bible stories rather than the Bible text. We got to know stories about Abraham and Moses and so on but never the text from which the stories were drawn.

Part of what hampered things at that time was that the normal translation was the Douay Version which is so garbled that it is very difficult to make any sense of it at all. When I joined the Dominicans after I left school, we did have the advantage of having a young teacher. He himself had been almost kicked out of training for the priesthood because he spent all his time studying the Bible instead of theology – an interesting concept! But he had a tremendous love for it and a tremendous enthusiasm, and in fact spent quite a bit of time at the Ecole Biblique in Jerusalem studying there, and we got him in his first flush of enthusiasm when he came back from that. I can remember listening to some of his classes and then rushing back to my room, picking up my Bible and trying to do the same sort of thing and I just couldn't begin. And it took me quite a long time to get past that first stage of actually knowing how to get into this conversation with the text so that the text was saying interesting things or challenging things to me. And that was a fairly dry time, which, with a bit of perseverance, I began to get somewhere with.

Then in the late sixties I was at a conference centre and we did a lot of work with youth groups, mainly school leavers, very often sixth form groups preparing for A-Level. And they said to us, 'We're doing A-Level Scripture and it's just another dry A-Level academic subject and it should be something different, can you help?' So we decided to put on courses, and that was, I suppose, what really got me into the Bible . . .

The start of studying Bible with other people is something which really grew out of that and it's something which I found extremely valuable because it's very easy, certainly from the tradition which I come from, to get by without noticing the presuppositions that one's carrying . . . What I found very interesting was one session that Howard [Cooper] and I did together at Spode on the beginning of Genesis. I entitled the leaflet advertising the thing: 'The Fall', and Howard very gently said to me, 'but that isn't a notion within Judaism'. And so it opened up a whole area of looking at texts without the presuppositions that I was carrying, which again was a very valuable thing . . .

I suppose in all of that what Jonathan was saying about a conversation is what comes through to me most. It's something which I find stimulating in coming to the Bible, in two ways. If I'm beset with problems and things I am trying to think about I come to the Bible, and as you said, I come looking for answers and simply find more questions which make me look at the thing in more and different ways. But the other thing I find is that if I spend time in actually studying the Bible hard and allowing myself to be confronted by the questions of the Bible I don't feel as if I need to go off for a time of prayer, because I feel that has already been prayer. So although in Christian tradition, 'prayerful reading of the Bible', *lectio divina*, was something which I'd heard about, it wasn't until I got into study of the Bible that that became a reality.

Athalaya Brenner I went to university in 1967 [in Israel]. It was the Six Day War. I wanted to major in English Linguistics and English Lit. Unfortunately at the time you couldn't major in one subject, you had to have two. The natural thing for me would have been to take Oriental studies, but this is what I did at school, so I decided, what the hell! I know nothing about Bible, I'll do it. And that was my first year, and then came the war, and we got back all our holy places and the war's hysteria, and I didn't know what people were talking about. And people said, 'these are *our* places, you know, it's in the Bible'. So I said, fine, I'll go down to that book, I'll read the passages, I'll see what makes those places ours – you know, almost exclusively ours. I'll see why I myself get so excited.

And I read those passages and they didn't do much for me on the nationalistic level. Neither did they do much for me on the religious level because I come from a household that is slightly observant but not religious at all. I've had no religious education. There was an abstract notion of a belief in God.

I've always found it very difficult to justify my identity – what am I? A Jewish person? An Israeli? What is an Israeli? Is it connected with the land? Is it connected with going to the army? Is it connected with fulfilling duties, having rights? What is it? It's always been a very strange animal for me. Some of my friends knew the answer. Some of them knew that they were Israelis but not Jewish. My generation, the generation that was born in Israel, went to the army, went to youth movement, went to kibbutz – they knew they were Israelis, they were not Jewish. I didn't know. I didn't know what the difference was. I didn't know what to tie it to. And while I was doing English and Bible and going through that terrible period, you know the post-Six Day War period when some of us, especially of radical views, could already see the trouble growing, and having more and more identity problems, and knowing exactly where things were going, I was dealing with the Bible and my anger was growing because I said to myself, it's such a nationalistic document.

It is there! Never mind the spirituality and religion and religiosity. The main thing for me was the use this was being put to.

So finally, when the time came to decide what I was doing, was I going to do a Masters in English or in Bible, I remember very consciously saying to myself, 'I'm not going to leave this text alone. I'm going to study this text. I'm going to use it.' What am I going to use it for? I'm going to use it, number one, to sidestep the issue, my personal issue, because for me to decide what I am, what is my identity, in a time of transition . . . I found this was impossible. So instead of deciding on that identity, I'm going to leech on to the text. In other words perform a displacement or a dislocation of sorts. And I'm going to redeem it at least for me . . . And there was a lot of anger in my decision and there still is. And later on when I added the feminist issue to my interests, I went through an intense period of anger, and I love being angry – it's good for me, it does things for me, I get places when I use my anger. And now its becoming different again because I'm less angry, and I've stuck with it because it stops me from losing an operating identity for something I haven't yet found. Neither do I think that I'll find it. I use it as a pretext and it feels comfortable and interesting.

Francis Landy   I don't think the history of how I came to Bible is very important. It was a chance and a very, very lucky chance that I found my way here, that I found the medium in which I can write. I think that what's happened in this writing is what draws me, which is the sense of meeting with something in the text that is me, that speaks me, that calls me, that belongs to that which is beyond it. And this is a kind of place. In fact, it is that which punctures that sense of emptiness, that meeting, at least for me.

Now the reason that I'm speaking now is because of what Athalya was saying, what Philip was saying – the sense first of all of that which endlessly deconstructs itself, that is so clear, so honest, so always capable of seeing the other side of itself that it reaches out beyond all religious constructions.

And then on to what Athalya was saying. One of my formative moments with the Bible was my first Bendorf [Bible Week], in which we were doing First Samuel. And having spent my time busily trying to understand the Song of Songs, I was forced to encounter this God who was a total monster and destroyed everybody in that story, and also created symbolic, nationalistic enemies like the Amalekites, in the way that Jews were nationalistic enemies and

Amalekites here [in Germany]. There was an extraordinary out-
burst of anger which led to me discarding religiosity in Eveline's
sense, and brought me very close to Athalya's place, anger which
mellowed partially because being angry all the time is rather boring,
but even more . . . because of something in the Bible that calls me,
that entrances me, and that is quintessentially Jewish no matter
what, which is its playfulness! Maybe it is different understandings
of what 'religious' means, but there is something in the Bible that
takes the religious dance – defences, rejections, abstractions, ways
of making oneself self-important, and takes them, plays with them,
makes them here and now, makes them part of the human
endeavour, the human delight in this world. And that's what I
love . . .

Gabriel Josipovici I think I'll add something to what one of you
has just been saying about why you feel happier about Bible is
because it's nearer to other texts. Because unlike most people here,
I came to the Bible very late and through a lot of other literary texts,
and for me its importance is not intrinsically greater than others.
Perhaps I can elaborate on that a little bit.

I suppose everybody has a sense of what they want to do in life
when they're young and then there comes a moment when this is
crystallized for them and it changes from being a general feeling, or
something you tell your parents' friends or whatever when they ask
you, to a clear sense of what it is. I'd always wanted to write, to write
fiction, but the moment when I saw that it was possible was after
reading Proust at seventeen, and this was a real watershed in my
existence. It's something that I keep going back to and that perhaps
plays the sort of role in my life that Bible played in Gordian's life.
And one of the things that Proust says in an essay, when he's going
into a dialogue with Ruskin – he doesn't like Ruskin's fetishism of
literature, where Ruskin has translated the religious impulse from
religion to art – Proust is very unhappy about this and he says, for
him it's wrong to think of works of art as great monuments, they're
thresholds. Those works of art which are most meaningful to us, he
says, are those which take us a certain way then leave us, having
shown us a road. And I suddenly realized of course this was what
had meant so much for me. Proust somehow made it possible for me
to fulfil what I had till then vaguely wanted to do, which was to
write. I wasn't going to write like him but he made it, like a good
teacher, possible for me to discover how to write for myself.

I realize that, in a way, my relation to other works that I came across, human artefacts of all kinds, has always been selfish, in the sense that the ones that I responded to were those that I could *use*, that could lead me, that opened a road and showed me that that was the way. There were many of these in the next ten, fifteen years, and it was a long time before I added the Bible to those.

It's not terribly interesting how that came about. I'd always been told Bible stories as a child, but hadn't really read the Bible, didn't come from a religious family. I'd never been inside a synagogue or church, taken my barmitzvah or anything like that. When I started to be a student at Oxford and to read literature, English literature, of course, was Christian, by and large, and therefore the kind of religious crisis one goes through as an adolescent, was always in terms of: does one convert to Christianity? Judaism didn't enter into it, it didn't seem at all meaningful. And then, of course, that quietens down, one forgets about this and gets on to the things one is really concerned with. But for some reason I'd started reading the Bible then for myself, got quite interested in it.

And then, as some of the people here have been saying already, I started to teach a course at Sussex [University] . . . on 'The Bible and English Literature', because when I was a student at Oxford everyone always said, 'you can't understand any literature, at least before 1800, unless you know the Bible'. But no one made any attempt to fill the gap! . . . Very quickly it became clear to me that I couldn't teach this with any sort of seriousness unless I knew some Hebrew . . . The beauty of Hebrew, as opposed to Latin, is that one can start reading the greatest literature in the language quite quickly . . .

So that has gone on, and as I read that, and as I became interested in Jewish matters, growing out of that, it was always this sense that, like Proust and Wallace Stevens and Dante, the writers who'd meant a lot to me because they'd opened a way, the Bible was doing just the same thing. It perhaps did it in different ways, possibly it will do it more often than they will. So far in my experience, my love for it and my desire to go on discovering it, is not essentially different from that . . .

Arthur Lelyveld   To introduce a different note, the Bible has not been and is not my primary academic interest. The focus of my interest had been in the first place the preparation for a Rabbinic career and my studies have largely taken me into Rabbinic thought . . .

The fact is however, that as a journeyman preacher for fifty years, I certainly was drawn to the biblical text and of course following the *parashat hashavua*, the portion of the week, and the *haftarah* [companion reading from the prophetic writings], I was familiar, forced to be familiar, with every aspect of *tenakh*. But my major interest has been not in *tenakh* as a whole but in the prophets, and that can be explained by the fact that there was an unusually splendid array of biblical scholars at the Hebrew Union College in Cincinatti when I was a student there . . . I was inspired by these men and the interesting thing is that each of these men was most interested in the prophetic aspect of biblical tradition. They were thorough biblical scholars, but they were excited most about the prophets. When I was invited back some twenty years ago to give the Goldenson lecture, which is an annual series of lectures at the Hebrew Union College-Jewish Institute of Religion, on the prophets of Israel, I chose as my subject 'The Social Relevance of the Eighth Century Prophets'. This has been where my interest has been. It has been a combination of general social concern, and my career in the Rabbinate has been dealing in great part with social problems and the prophets as the foundation and inspiration for Jewish social concern.

Judith Elkan   If I begin by saying that we are here to study Isaiah, [I think of] the words *nahamu nahamu ammi* 'comfort, comfort, my people' (Isa. 40.1) . . . My love for words has been in all the three languages that I've grown up with. My first language, my mother tongue, is Arabic, my next language was Hebrew and the third English. I am always tremendously moved and excited when I hear the chanting of Sephardic melodies . . . and that must go back to the chanting that was in my house, which I don't remember but which I think is there without conscious memories. It would have been the chanting in a very Orthodox home of parents who came from Syria and where . . . the Song of Songs is chanted every Friday evening. That kind of excitement about words and about the resonance and reverberation of the biblical text I think have stayed with me always.

My education led away from Israel, where I was born, to England and to going to an English school where Hebrew got left behind . . . I went back to Israel in 1948 and entered some kind of dialogue with the language and with the religion because I was sucked into my very religious family, clan . . . But inside me . . . there was always a situation of being at the interface of what my logical mind told me, and my logical mind was moving away from religion and an explanation of life and the world, and this sense that I belonged there . . . I came to psychology and the idea that I wanted to do something in the world of psychotherapy and children, and discovered that I badly needed to understand myself and the complexities of my life and needed to have some analysis. The short and long of it is that all these accidents of life led me to England . . . and I ended up at the Tavistock Clinic where I did a training in psychoanalytical work with children and adolescents . . .

Then a number of happy accidents led to my meeting with Jonathan . . . at the home on a Tuesday evening of a man called Rabbi Sperber. Rabbi Sperber is a man who would take a text and study it in an evening with a whole group of people . . . He was a very inspiring person. I think he was the embodiment for me of someone who was very humane. There was the quintessence of humanity about him. A beautiful way of approaching a text and opening it up and an openness to everybody's ideas who were present and a receptivity about him. It inspired me greatly and when he moved to Jerusalem I always went to the same Tuesday evening that he maintained in Jerusalem . . .

Then Jonathan . . . asked me to give a talk to the Leo Baeck College students on the *parashah*, [the weekly portion] on Joseph and Potiphar's wife . . . Eventually I overcame my reticence and I said 'yes'.

So in a very scared way I decided that I just have to read the text myself and see what I could make of it, and I really was very scared. I read it again and again and again. Then I think this very exciting thing that Philip referred to occurred, where suddenly from within the text itself and very much not with any idea that I was going to say something psychoanalytic about the text, I found myself really becoming immersed in it, becoming interested in it, becoming interested in reading around the text. In a sense it was psycho-analytic in that there's the text and the context. What I think is psychoanalytic – in my reading of psychoanalysis and the connec-tion between the biblical text and a dream text or a psychoanalytic session – is the connecting through steeping oneself in the text with the mood, with the meaning that emerges as you stay with the text or with the situation, while relinquishing preconceptions about it and letting it take over . . .

I think that one of the important things that I feel about this approach is that it isn't reductionist. I don't approach a text with a psychoanalytic idea that this text can be interpreted in that way . . . But somewhere there has to be a matching which may have then a fertilizing consequence . . . the text itself and some psychoanalytic idea can actually generate something new . . . So I think I look at the text as something to explore and be creative with.

The other thing I haven't said for me is the beauty of this text . . . and there's an image in my mind that's always been there about the Hebrew words . . . It feels as though each word is like a stone, like the stones of Jerusalem, and locked in each of these are so many levels of meaning . . . So I do feel that somehow this text is inspirational because of the particular characteristics of the Hebrew language . . .

[The psychoanalyst Wilfrid] Bion talked about relinquishing memory and desire; and to give it an extreme form he said, you should come to your session not thinking about your patient's history, not even thinking about your patient's age, not even thinking whether your patient is a man or a woman . . . What he really meant was that you might come to a session and actually know in your mind that your patient is a thirty-three-year-old and a man, an accountant and so on, but at that moment in your session you might not be meeting a thirty-three-year-old patient, and you might not be meeting a man and you might be meeting the voice of a three-month or a three-year-old little girl or . . . that's what might be present. So how to actually be present with the emotional phenomenon that is taking place and allow it to be formed first of all, from being wordless . . .

From that point of view then, you might come to a text in the same way, as you might come to a session. Where you would really expect that things would occur in a psychoanalytic session as with a text, that couldn't have ever occurred, that could only occur uniquely through the meeting of two minds in a particular time. Which could never have occurred if those two particular minds hadn't met and hadn't met, of course, in a very sequestred setting. In that sense the meeting with the text is also of a kind, because if we struggle with a text we're often doing it in a very lonely way, we are alone, struggling with it, bringing ourselves to it.

Howard Cooper   Its always the therapists who speak at the end! There seem so many different themes to pick up, maybe I have to take a step back. I think I came to biblical texts through Jonathan. That's a very straightforward statement. Through studying at the Leo Baeck College and learning the difference between exegesis and eisegesis which I think Jonathan taught me. But, what I'm now feeling and realizing is that, of course, it's always eisegesis. I've begun to realize that the understanding that there is a meaning there in the text is a kind of fantasy. The meaning is always beyond. And that's what brings together for me working with a patient and working with a text – it is realizing what I can actually understand from what is there in the narrative that is spoken. I'm always only going to be outside it, I'm always going to be grasping after something that is beyond me. That's what I love about working with patients, that's what I love about working with the text; it seems to me that capacity to glimpse insights into a kind of truthfulness of feeling or truthfulness of perception that is possible in those intimate encounters with texts, with the texts of *tenakh* and with the texts of people. But they are elusive and they go beyond.

So I've learned from Jonathan a sensitivity to language, and also from Francis, which I carry then into my work with people and listening to what is actually said, and not what I think is going to be said or I want to be said, but what is actually said, and trying to stay with that, with what is actually said in the text. And then bringing to bear on it all sorts of my own ideas and fantasies and thoughts and whatever. And that meeting is very exciting. That's one way of talking about my engagement with texts.

Another way would be to say that I feel that the biblical text . . . and particularly the narrative sections of the Bible, are the incarnation of the Jewish myth, and in them I can see where I have come from in some kind of collective way. They contain stories which are so alien and so distant and so far away as to be completely beyond belief and at the same time they are talking about situations which are personal and which relate to me. And I love that ambiguity that they are both utterly beyond anything I experience and they are also very close.

I think part of my work is to rescue those texts from what's been done to them and to make them accessible to Jews and also to Christians – because I do a lot of work, partly with Gordian, partly elsewhere – rescuing these texts from a kind of narrowness of perception which has been imposed on them over the years, which has in a way strangled the religiosity out of them. I think it is part of my work to give the texts back to people who need them and want them because I think that this contact with the myth is really crucial. I'm using myth in the sense of that kind of perception of reality in a symbolic form that we need, and that without it we do become neurotic. I mean we can become neurotic with it as well, but for me the biblical stories do somehow encapsulate a kind of truthfulness of perception.

What I wonder is if I'd come to Shakespeare first would I also be feeling exactly the same way. I don't know. Or Proust. I may do. Whether the great literary artistic works are able to capture this essence of truthfulness? Maybe all great art does that. But certainly for me the Bible is great art . . . and that literary approach which is more than just a literary approach, is for me really crucial.

I remember a study session that Francis gave on the Ten Commandments at the Leo Baeck College when I was a student, in which you talked about God saying that He was a jealous God and you said something there about this being the beginning of the long and monotonous history of God's possessiveness. I can't remember exactly how you said it, but there was *suddenly* a moment of illumination. Yes, of course, God is just another character. But . . . I think there has to be a 'but' at the end of that sentence, but somehow it helped me to free myself from having to maintain God as the 'religious' figure in the story. That somehow the religiosity is about the relationship between the characters and the tension between the characters. Holding that tension is for me connected to the tension between opposites, a very Jungian idea. That that's what the text seemed always to do to defy that reductiveness. I don't know that that's 'always' – I'm very selective in my reading.

Gordian Marshall One or two things are running around in my mind listening to this. One is that I think the word 'religion' or 'religiosity' is being used in different ways by different people in the group. For some, I think, it may be the structure of religion which I would also not want to tie in too closely with the Bible. And we've got to be freed in a way from the structures of thought that religions have dumped on us, sometimes in order to come to terms with the Bible. But at the same time for me, I think there's a sense of religion which is truer of the Bible than any of the religious structures that I know; that is a contact with something which is beyond us and yet more real. And that links in with the question of the fundamentalist reading of texts which is problematic in many areas in all our traditions. For me, I think, fundamentalism has to be a selective literalism, not just a literalism, but a selective literalism. Because, as Howard said, if you set one text against another, you can't come away saying, 'well that's clearly what's being said', because for me part of the richness of the Bible is there are so many contradictions, and as soon as you begin to think, yes, that's what it's saying, something else hits you and you say, no!, think again.

But part of what's been worrying in my brain during the conversation is why is it that I give such importance to this text, rather than as Howard said, to Shakespeare or something else. One thing of it is, yes it is good literature, but there are parts of the Bible that are not. They are clumsy. I can't just say that they have their weight because they're good literature, because they're not. They wouldn't stand up against some other things, and yet I give them a weight. I'm prepared to argue with them. I'm prepared to be challenged by them in a way which in another writer I would say, 'OK, that's his opinion, it's not mine'. But I can't leave the Bible in that way. Part of it is, I suppose, a belief in some sense of revelation, that in a way God is speaking through the text. Not that God is dictating the text, but God's voice can be heard through the text. But then, looking at friends who have other scriptures, Koran or, with Sikhs or Hindus other scriptures are there, and for them that same conversation often seems to work, as works between me and the Bible. So in a way, there's a level at which the presence of God in the text is the presence of God which I place in the text, which then speaks back to me . . .

Gabriel Josipovici   I just want to say a word about authority and literature. It seems to me that with a writer one becomes committed to, say Kafka, it's not really a question of saying, 'yes, you know, this is rather a beautiful passage, this is a less beautiful passage'. Everything they said, every letter, takes on a significance and a meaningfulness. I don't see anything intrinsically different in how one might feel in relation to the Bible.

Gordian Marshall   All I was saying is that I treat the Bible differently from the way I treat any other author.

Philip Davies   Who is the author of the Bible? That's part of the charm. You don't really know who you're reading.

Jonathan Magonet   Perhaps that is a good word with which to end!

—— 4 ——

'Open rebuke and hidden love'

I want to begin this chapter with a passage that I find very moving and ultimately somewhat daunting. It comes from the writings of one of the foremost Orthodox Jewish thinkers of this century, Joshua Dov Soloveitchik. In his book *Halakhic Man*, he explores what it means today, in this complex, secular world to be someone committed to traditional religious values and more specifically one bound by the *halakhah*, Jewish law. He includes in this work some autobiographical remarks, including an account of what it was like to grow up in a religious household in which the great Jewish teachers of the past were not merely names, but in some sense living presences in the home. Thus his father would conduct study sessions on the works of the Rambam (the acronym for Rabbi Moses ben Maimon, Maimonides, 1135–1204) and have to defend the great teacher's often unexpected and controversial decisions against the attacks of his classical critics, whose arguments were taken up by others in the room. He writes:

> I understood not a word of the subject, but two impressions fixed themselves in my innocent young brain: (1) The Ramban was surrounded by opponents and 'enemies' who wanted to harm him; (2) Father was his only defender. Who knows what would have happened to him without father?
>
> (Sometimes) I would go broken-hearted to my mother: 'Mother, Daddy can't explain the Rambam! What shall we do?' 'Don't worry,' Mother would say. 'Father will find an answer for the Rambam. And if he can't, perhaps when you grow up you will find an answer for the Rambam. The main thing is to keep on learning Torah, and to enjoy it and let it excite you.

Soloveitchik goes on to explain the consequences of this child-hood experience:

This was no golden daydream of a young child. It was a psychological and historical reality which even today lives in the depths of my soul. When I sit and learn I find myself at once in the company of the wise men of tradition, and our relationship is a personal one. The Rambam is on my right, Rabbenu Tam on the left, Rashi sits in front and explains, Rabbenu Tam fires questions, Rambam makes decisions, Raavad criticizes. All of them are in my little room . . . They look at me with affection, join in reasoning and *gemara*, support and encourage me like a father.

The learning of Torah is not merely a didactic exercise . . . but the powerful expression of a love that crosses the generations, a marriage of spirits, a unity of souls. Those who hand down the Torah meet in one inn of history with those who receive it.[1]

I find this very moving as I have come to experience something of the joy of studying in this manner. I suppose I am also envious that my own childhood experience of Judaism, let alone Jewish study, was so utterly different.

It is worth spending a moment reviewing that, if only to correct the impression that all Jewish children are brought up with this richness.

My earliest memories of Jewish learning are more painful. Sunday school at my local Orthodox synagogue in south London. The fact of it's being in south London already says something. Whereas the Jewish community of north London is large, tight, not to say claustrophobic in some ways, those who lived south of the river during and immediately after the war were more isolated from each other, perhaps to a large extent by choice. They were part of the second generation of Jews whose parents, from Poland or Russia at the turn of the century, still belonged to the old culture, but wished their children to succeed in this new world. The price paid for this was often a marginal attachment to Judaism accompan-ied by a strong success ethic, often expressed through entry into the professions, especially medicine and law. Their relationship with the synagogue was ambiguous to say the least. It might be parodied

[1]From *Ish Hahalakha*, Jerusalem 1979, pp. 230f. trans. Norman Solomon, *Spirituality and Prayer*, Paulist Press 1983.

by a familiar view that they joined for burial rights, attended only
once a year, for the Jewish High Holydays, and really kept up
contacts out of respect (guilt?) for their parents. That was their
choice, but those who suffered, at least so we experienced it at the
time, were their children (especially the boys) who knew little of
Jewish content at home, but were expected to attend classes at the
synagogue on Sunday, sometimes even (heaven forbid) on Tuesday
and Thursday evenings as well, in preparation for their barmitzvah at
thirteen. Since this could only take place if they passed an exam, at
least in theory, there was considerable pressure to attend – and a
concomitant sense of freedom when the whole business was over.
Very few stayed on after thirteen, and in a sad way there is a
generation of Jews who are religiously crippled, with a great deal of
residual resentment, a highly selective and largely unused anthology
of Jewish knowledge and practice, and a thirteen-year-old God.

Classes were aimed at teaching us our *parashah*, the section from
the Torah, the Five Books of Moses, that we would chant in public
in synagogue at the barmitzvah ceremony, as well as the *haftarah*,
the parallel reading from the Prophets that accompanied it. To all
this were added a variety of blessings that had to be chanted before
and after these readings, which meant mastering not only the
Hebrew text (at least to the level of being able to read it aloud, even
if one did not really understand it) but also the different chants. A
lot depended on the teachers, on whether the home atmosphere was
supportive (or merely neurotic) about the whole process, and the
self-consciousness or lack of it of the boy. I was personally
inordinately shy, terrified of reading aloud in front of anyone, and
frequently given to bursting into tears out of sheer anxiety. What
made things worse at the time was that my father, coming from
Canada, had a different, 'Russian', melody for the chanting which
he had learnt from his own father, and which (quite rightly I now
see) he wanted me to know. The problem was that it differed from
the 'German' melody we used at the synagogue, and I had to master
two tunes, which was bad enough, but be *different* from the others,
an awful burden for someone who desperately wanted to be
inconspicuously the *same*.

In the event I only had to do the haftarah, which I managed to
stumble through without actually breaking into tears. (My mother
was certainly in tears afterwards, and probably my father as well –
but out of sheer relief rather than for the usual more sentimental
reasons.)

My father had argued that knowing the *haftarah* was more important than the Torah reading because I might always be called upon to chant it again in later years, an idea that filled me with dread at the time. He would be called upon many times a year to do so in his own synagogue because of that very special melody and his marvellous way of chanting it. I once got to chant it in one of the synagogues in East Berlin, which was literally to invade the area of the 'German' melody. They were very polite about it.

Of my teachers at Sunday school I remember one young man whom the children teased mercilessly; the headmaster, whom we called names and viewed with considerable fear, though I today would rather like to be able to know him; two tiny elderly spinster ladies, the Misses Cohen, who were very sweet and gave me the first lessons; and an older man, nicknamed 'clump Cohen', because he had an artificial arm which, so rumour had it, he would swing at the heads of misbehaving children. In terms of content, all I remember is repeating the same Bible stories (usually from Genesis, but suitably edited) year in and out as we seemed to start from the same place in each new class; the endless rote learning of the same bits of the Bible in Hebrew; and perhaps some grammar as well – I somehow kept the slim green Hebrew primer in which I'd written my name and address, locating it in Europe, the World and the Cosmos. It may even be that the Sunday school had a well-organized programme of studies, well taught and administered – but little of it remained except a complex about reading Hebrew aloud that stayed with me well into my years at Rabbinic seminary, and a feeling of utter confusion about the relationship between the odd bits of information we picked up about Judaism and any real values applicable in the world 'out there'. I suspect that I learned more actual Bible stories from a comic strip Bible that my father obtained from the United States which I used to read surreptitiously in synagogue during the service.

But behind these odd memories and obvious difficulties were a number of deeper problems that were affecting the whole Jewish world. I experienced them in distressing ways precisely in this childhood world where the problem of the continuity of Jewish life and tradition was being explored and tested out.

For example, we were always being cajoled, bullied or bribed (stamps for attendance, sweets on various occasions, prizes for good conduct!) into keeping the ritual law. This meant, in particular, *kashrut*, the eating of food in accordance with the dietary

laws. The trouble was that my family, already somewhat assimil-
ated, living in a part of London without many Jewish facilities, and
not a little concerned about the cost of kosher meat, had become
rather casual about keeping a proper kosher home. (When my *buba*
(grandmother) came all the way from Canada to attend my
barmitzvah, we suddenly went into convulsions at home, throwing
out the old and completely restocking with new sets of crockery,
cutlery and cooking utensils, so that she could keep *kashrut* to her
own very strict standards.) But when asked in the Sunday school if
we kept it properly, I had to be honest and confess that we did not,
an awesome conflict at the time. The same applied to travelling on
the Sabbath. Driving a car is forbidden by traditional Jewish law,
and this is one thing that determines where Orthodox Jews locate
their homes in relationship to the synagogue. But this too was no
longer something that bothered my family and had to be admitted
(or confessed) in public. (Again *buba's* arrival caused trouble as she
insisted on walking to synagogue, a couple of miles, despite her 'bad
feet'. So I had to accompany her along Acre Lane, seemingly for
hours, so as to sit for yet more hours in the synagogue and repeat the
process home. That stubborn heroism is magnificent. It infuriated
my father who had left that world firmly behind, and it further
alienated me from the whole business.)

Incidentally I was amused to hear about my old synagogue some
years later one of those apocryphal stories that somehow say it all.
One Day of Atonement, the holiest and most solemn day of the
Jewish calendar, when everyone turns up but driving is also
forbidden, the police sent a message into the Rabbi. They had a
problem. It seems that the whole of Brixton High Road was
chock-a-block full with cars parked everywhere, but none of them
were in the synagogue car park where they ought to be. Could the
Rabbi explain this and do something about it? Of course he could
not explain that classical hypocrisy of parking the car round the
corner to pretend one had not driven. But it does highlight the
paradoxes of a tradition at odds with itself and the world around it.

If I may be forgiven another brief excursus, there is a story of two
au pairs talking about their respective families. The one staying in a
Jewish home explains that they have these odd religious festivals. In
one of them they eat in the dining room, but smoke in the
bathroom. In another they smoke in the dining room but eat in the
bathroom. In yet another they eat and smoke in the bathroom.
(Though it looses something in the explaining: On Shabbat one eats

but may not smoke (causing a fire is a forbidden category of work); on Tisha B'Av, the ninth day of the month of Av, a day when we lament the destruction of the two Temples, one works as usual, but fasts; Yom Kippur, the Day of Atonement, is both a fast day and a 'day of rest'. An au pair's view of Jewish customs would probably make for a more honest book than much that is written about Jewish family life.

Perhaps if I had had some real feeling of the importance of these rituals during my childhood (beyond a sense of the awful restrictions they seemed to impose) I might have found a way of coping with the contradictions between the theory and the practice. But they were, and in some ways remain, the points at which the maintenance of a separate Jewish identity becomes tested in a gentile environment. We were all caught up in the transition between two cultures. Our loyalty to the past was severely tested, precisely because it was based on habits of behaviour, largely discarded, without the concomitant learning needed to give them value and meaning. We could only experience them as inconveniences to our integration in this wider world.

So I am not a little jealous of Soloveitchik's experience.

Nevertheless the world he describes is daunting because anyone coming to it from the outside has an enormous distance to cross, both to acquire the basic knowledge and to find an environment with the same qualities. The figures he names, with the exception of Rashi, are primarily concerned not with Bible but with Talmud and *halakhah*, that is to say the 'legal' tradition in all its forms. Bible is not studied in quite this hot-house way, but the debate is nevertheless there to be experienced on the pages of the great Rabbinic editions of the Bible, the *miqraot gedolot* (literally the 'great scriptures').

A page of the Rabbinic Bible is already pretty daunting. It looks rather like an architect's blueprint except that the large enclosed spaces that should represent rooms are instead blocks of print. Towards the top right hand corner of a double page spread is a vertical rectangle of print containing, in the largest letters on the page, the actual verses to be discussed, rarely more than a dozen at most. (The Pentateuch alone takes up two volumes, each the size of a telephone directory.) To the left of this block is a narrower one, with smaller print, containing the Targum Onkelos, the 'official' aramaic translation of the passage. Between these in the narrow gap of white space are various Hebrew letters denoting particular instructions about the setting out of the masoretic text itself, including words that are to be spelled in a particular way, unusual or unexpected words that the scribe might miswrite. Just to complete the 'targums', since there were a number of different ones, some fragments of others are also printed at the top of the left-hand page in certain editions.

So far so good in that all of these things are still printed in the normal square Hebrew characters and have full punctuation, and in the case of the text itself, the musical notations that also divide up the sentences into their smaller sense units. But the rest of the page is printed in a quite different type-face known as 'Rashi script', not because the great Bible commentator wrote in that script but because it was adopted for the first printed editions of the Hebrew Bible, which inevitably had Rashi's commentary attached to it. Subsequently the same type face was adopted for all the other commentaries as well. Incidentally, at this point all the printing also gets very small – and some portable editions of the Rabbinic Bible are guaranteed to induce eyestrain from an early age.

The presence of the targum is because of the tradition, ultimately going back to the Bible itself, of insisting that the text be read in public clearly and explicitly with an explanation if necessary. The targum in Aramaic, which was the vernacular language of the early rabbinic period, was read alongside the biblical passages in the synagogue to ensure that people understood the reading. Its inclusion in the Rabbinic Bible is more a reflection of its testimony to the earliest official translation/interpretation of the text, and Rashi will frequently quote it as giving the correct meaning of a particular text. Just to complete the 'textual-critical' information available on the page, there are more extensive masoretic notes, often located just beneath the major block of the biblical text and a selection from a vast cross-referencing system, the *toledot aharon*, which indicates where the verse in question is also discussed in the pages of the Talmud, the major collections of Midrash (Rabbinic exegesis of the Bible) and even the mystical work the Zohar. (A Cambridge theology student visiting Leo Baeck College noted that he now understood the difference between us. 'At Cambridge we are interested in the newest commentary; at Leo Baeck you are interested in the oldest ones!')

If all the above provide the essential tools for the traditional scholar, the rest of the double page is filled with the commentaries of the great mediaeval exegetes. Rashi (the acronym taken from the initial letters of his name Rabbi Shlomo ben Yitzhak, 1040–1105, France, studied in Worms, Germany) takes pride of place often on the inner side of the page, the top of his commentary sometimes being laid out like an inverted 'L' along the top of the page as well. In other editions he may sit as a broad block of text across the whole page just beneath the Bible text itself.

In more or less the equivalent place on the left-hand facing page (remembering, of course that Hebrew books read from right to left so that the right hand page is read first) is the commentary of Abraham Ibn Ezra, (1089–1140, born in Spain, but he travelled widely in North Africa and Europe) whose remarks are often so cryptic that some two hundred 'super-commentaries' to this works were already completed in his lifetime – one of which usually sits below him on the same page in even smaller print.

Above Ibn Ezra you may find the Baal Haturim (Jacob ben Asher, 1270–1340). The name this time is not an acronym but reflects another Rabbinic habit of naming someone after their major literary work, in this case the *'Arbaah Turim'*, the 'four rows' or 'sections' into which he organized the first major mediaeval compilation of Jewish law. His Bible commentary is actually a mystical one based to some extent on *gematria*, the use of the numerical values of the Hebrew letters to compare words that add up to the same number. It is perhaps a little ironic that he sits above the highly rationalistic Ibn Ezra who was less than happy with such methods.

Beneath Rashi on the right hand page and often extending on to the left one as well beneath Ibn Ezra is Ramban (Rabbi Moses ben Nahman or Nahmanides, 1194–1270, Spain, Palestine), not to be confused with Moses ben Maimon, Maimonides, Soloveitchik's 'Rambam'. In his commentary he will often begin by quoting Rashi or Ibn Ezra before arguing against them and offering his own view. (When Professor Jacob Licht checked each of Ramban's 632 individual comments on the Pentateuch he found that he quoted Rashi in 37.7% of them and Ibn Ezra in 12.8%.) He prefaced his commentary to Genesis with a little poem from which the title of this chapter is derived. He states as part of his intention in writing his commentary that he would argue with great respect with the master, Rashi, and with Ibn Ezra he would have 'open rebuke and hidden love'. This remarkable phrase sums up precisely that respect for great teachers and the equal commitment to discover the truth as you yourself see it, even if it means arguing against them, that is at the heart of the true Rabbinic debate.

To complete our journey we should also mention Obadiah Sforno (c.1470–c.1550) who sits beneath Ibn Ezra. He was an Italian Jewish physician and philosopher, and the teacher of Johann Reuchlin, the Christian defender of Jews and Jewish literature.

Finally, and, to keep it in the family, beneath him on the same left hand page is the Rashbam (Rabbi Samuel ben Meir, c.1080–c.1174, France), who is the grandson of Rashi and often argues, though respectfully, with his grandfather!

Other editions may add other commentators, but if we are to enter their world we must now look at something of what they said.

At first glance Rashi, who is the Jewish Bible commentator *par excellence*, may disappoint. If you go with your own questions about a particular passage or sentence, you may not find it answered, and instead encounter a detailed discussion of the grammar of a particular word, a note that he agrees with the targum, a cryptic comment that does not seem to make much sense or a brief excursion into the midrash. The trick with Rashi, and I, like countless thousands of others owe this knowledge to a remarkable Bible teacher in Jerusalem Nechama Leibowitz, is to ask yourself: what is the problem in the text that Rashi has seen? That 'problem' may be the unusual juxtaposition of two words or sentences, an odd grammatical form, a contradiction with another passage elsewhere or any of a number of other difficulties inherent in the text. To this 'problem' Rashi brings his own answer, either in terms of the '*pshat*', the plain, common sense meaning of the text, or from the rich world of Rabbinic midrash – but he seems to take for granted that you saw the same problem so he does not have to explain what it was. The effect of Rashi is thus to teach us a whole new way of reading, something very similar to the 'close reading' that has been applied to Bible in recent years by literary scholars. He sensitizes us to the nuances of the Hebrew, to the lacunae in the text, to seeming redundancies and repetitions, to the various possibilities of meaning in a story we would otherwise gloss over. But for those exploring Judaism he also provides a highly accessible doorway into the world of midrash that lies at the heart of Jewish ethical and imaginative thought.

To give just one famous example of his ability to 'read' a text here is his view of God's words to Abraham in the famous story of the 'binding of Isaac' (Gen. 22):

Take, please, your son, your only one, whom you love, Isaac. (v. 22)

Rashi here follows the Midrash (Genesis Rabbah 55.7), the early Rabbinic commentary, in seeing in this simple statement something much more complicated, namely that it is only half of a conversation, the other half of which was not recorded. He proceeds to fill in the missing part as follows:

God: Take, please, your son.
Abraham: I have two sons.
God: Your only one.
Abraham: This one is the only son of his mother, and the other one (Ishmael) is the only son of his mother.
God: Whom you love.
Abraham: I love them both.
God: Isaac!

And why, continues Rashi, did God not say so at once? So as not to confuse Abraham suddenly lest his mind become disturbed and unbalanced.

Though Rashi has expressed this in terms of a dialogue which is not explicitly there in the text, he is actually only dramatizing for the sake of clarification something clearly present in the construction of the sentence. God's piling up of the descriptive terms for the son in question, when Abraham must have been aware from the beginning of who was intended, reflects Abraham's inner struggle. (In much the same way as Joseph overdid his protest when invited to sleep with Potiphar's wife.) Rashi draws our attention to this, but does it by introducing a Midrash with enormous style, subtlety and sensitivity to the implicit drama in what is happening.

Rashi steps off the pages of his commentary as a modest, quiet person, an impression reinforced by the number of places in which he acknowledges that he does not understand a particular text. His grandson, Rashbam, notes that his grandfather was continually revising his commentary in the light of new insights up until his death. Nor should one underestimate Rashi's phenomenal output for he also produced an indispensable commentary to most of the tractates of the Babylonian Talmud. His commentary also reflects his expertise in agricultural life, he was himself in the wine-growing business, and occasionally one hears through some particular comment the tragic situation of Jewish life in mediaeval France in the wake of the crusades.

But if Rashi is a saintly figure, Abraham Ibn Ezra is tempera-
mentally at the other extreme of the intellectual spectrum. A
physician, philosopher, astronomer, grammarian, poet, he typified
the 'renaissance' mind of the 'golden age' of Islamic Spain. His
commentary may range from the most cryptic, and indeed obscure,
comment about a particular word to a ten page discussion on the
reasons for the differences between the two versions of the Ten
Commandments (in Exodus and Deuteronomy) – a discussion that
applies rigorous logic to the problems of differences between them
and which dismisses simplistic traditional attempts to gloss over
them. Indeed from time to time he sails very close to the wind in his
interpretation, pausing to remark 'the one who understands will
know what I mean' without spelling out precisely what the full
implications are. Thus he identifies the break at the beginning of
chapter 40 of the Book of Isaiah as opening a new author and indeed
isolates the four passages in 'Second Isaiah' known to today's Bible
scholarship as the 'Servant Songs'. Indeed reading Ibn Ezra is often
an intellectual treat because he was essentially a scientist, utilizing
comparative philology (from Arabic), a vast reading of other
scholars, Jewish and Karaite, knowledge from a variety of other
disciplines of which he was master, to discover the truth of the text.
It is quite common to find Ibn Ezra refuting a view as improbable
that has turned up again in a twentieth century commentary – and it
is one of the curious lacunae in contemporary scholarship that until
very recently little if any attention was paid (either by Jewish or
Christian or 'secular' scholars) to his work or, for that matter, of any
of the mediaeval Jewish commentators. Above all, and this is a
characteristic of his commentary that I unashamedly enjoy, he
could be extremely cutting in his dismissal of the views of others.
For example when Exodus 23 discusses the case of someone's ox
goring the ox of his neighbour (v. 35) he informs us of a contemporary scholar who reads the verse to mean not the 'ox belonging to the
neighbour of the owner' but the 'neighbouring ox', the ox next to
the first ox. He refutes this view and adds that to the best of his
knowledge the only person who can claim to be the neighbour of an
ox is the scholar who made that particular remark.

What separates Ibn Ezra from Rashi, and indeed separates the
'French/German' from the 'Spanish' schools of commentary is the
same issue that divided earlier Rabbinic schools over the consequences for commentators of scripture being of divine origin. That
is to say, should it be treated as if every letter had overwhelming

significance since it came from God's mouth so that absolutely everything could legitimately be interpreted, or was the Bible like any other literary document to the extent that it had to be understood in terms of the rules of literary criticism. While Rashi tends largely, but not exclusively, to the former view, Ibn Ezra is strongly committed to the latter. Thus he will recognize 'poetic licence' in the writings of the prophets and not take such exaggerated language or metaphors at their face value. He notes, for example, the problem of attempting literally to 'circumcize the foreskins of your heart'.

In the matter of 'biblical parallelism', that poetic device whereby a half-line of verse is followed by a second half-line which says something similar in different words (a very subtle and complex subject to analyse) Rashi might see the need to interpret the second half as if it was a separate subject (for him no repetition was redundant). Ibn Ezra would merely note that the poet was saying the same thing in different words for poetic effect, and move on.

When confronted with differences in the two versions of the Ten Commandments, such as the fact that the Exodus version says '*remember* the Sabbath day' (Ex. 20.8) whereas the Deuteronomy version has '*keep* the Sabbath day' (Deut. 5.12), Jewish tradition has God utter the two simultaneously in a miraculous way. Ibn Ezra points out that this worthy tradition of the Rabbis should not become a new fundamentalism and be interpreted literally. He demonstrates that whereas God might be perfectly capable of saying two different words simultaneously, human beings would not be capable of hearing them simultaneously! To prove this he turns to the scientific observation that our senses record visual stimuli quicker than auditory ones – we see lightning before we hear the thunder. Thus sounds travel through the air to us in a sequence as they are made, each letter of a word following its predecessor. So if the two words arrived at the same time we would be totally confused by all the letters arriving at once. Instead he prefers to see the Deuteronomy version as Moses' recasting of the original Exodus version using other words and adding extra comments to clarify things. Thus 'remember' and 'keep' are to some extent synonymous (as he proves by again quoting contemporary psychological views on the location of memory in the human mind). He sums up this view in a phrase that brilliantly epitomizes this approach: 'As the soul is to the body, so is the meaning to the word.' Words may be changed provided their meaning is correctly conveyed – a major attack on biblical literalism.

As you will note it is with some reluctance that I move on from Ibn Ezra who must have been a devastating opponent but great company. I do so to bring Ramban into the fray as he takes on his two great masters. Again we enter a different world view. While Ibn Ezra was a wandering scholar for most of his life, Nahmanides was an establishment figure. A master of Jewish law he was also a mystic introducing this dimension to his biblical commentary. He is perhaps most renowned for defending Judaism against the attacks of Pablo Christiani, a converted Jew, in a famous disputation in Barcelona in 1263 before the King of Aragon. A full record of this dispute is extant and gives a fascinating record of the challenge and play of ideas. In the Jewish view Nahmanides won, but as a result was banished from Spain and at the age of 72 settled in Palestine living with the small, impoverished Jewish community there. He lived out the last few years of his life in exile and we have a record of his experiences through letters he wrote to his family. In what amounted to an ethical will to his oldest son, he wrote:

Read in the Torah regularly so that you may be able to fulfil it. When you rise from the book think carefully over what you have learned to see if there is something there to put into practice.

In the view of Solomon Schechter, 'Nahmanides represented Judaism from the side of emotions and feelings as Maimonides did from the side of reason and logic.'

I would like to bring a passage from the Ramban which illustrates how the three great masters meet in argument as Soloveitchik has described it. But before I do so I must point out that it will be no earth shattering experience. We have here three great minds, dedicated to clarifying the meaning of the central text of their tradition. They bring phenomenal gifts of intellect, scholarly disciplines and native wit, and their 'discussion' will ultimately cover the whole of the Pentateuch. To eavesdrop on just one passage is only to catch a glimpse of what is really at stake for them in this unending dialogue. The passage is not 'exciting', but it is a mysterious one from the earlier chapters of Genesis that try to spell out the development of the peoples of the world from the time of the creation.

Cush begat Nimrod who began to be a mighty one upon the earth. He was a mighty hunter before the Eternal, therefore it was said, 'like Nimrod a mighty hunter before the Eternal.' The beginning of his kingdom was Babel and Erech and Accad and Calneh in the land of Shinar. (Gen. 10.8–10)

Not the most promising of material and indeed somewhat obscure. What does 'mighty' (Hebrew *gibbor*, one who is powerful) mean in this context? It becomes clearer when it is added to the word for hunting, *tzaid*. Just as others are credited with introducing particular things in these primaeval histories, so Nimrod introduced hunting. But what does it mean that he did this 'before the Eternal'? Rashi comments on *gibbor tzaid*:

He ensnared the minds of men and stirred them up to rebel against God.

How on earth does he get there? First, and in this he is merely following the line of the Rabbis, he derives the name Nimrod from the root *marad* which actually means 'to rebel'. Since names in the Hebrew Bible are more than just chance labels we carry around with us, and often indicate something of the character or destiny of a particular person, it is reasonable to see in his name a judgment on his behaviour, if we accept this premise.

But it may be that something else is at work here as well because of the use of the word *tzaid*, 'hunt', which the Targum Onkelos actually omits to translate at all. In Genesis 25.28 the different attitudes of Isaac and Rebeccah to the twins Esau and Jacob are noted. 'Isaac loved Esau because of the game (our word *tzaid* again) in his mouth.' Presumably this means that Esau went hunting and provided his father with food that he liked, he literally put it in his father's mouth. But the Rabbis went against the obvious meaning of this verse and read it to the detriment of Esau – that he won the heart of his father through deception. It was in Esau's mouth, not in Isaac's, that the 'hunting' (i.e. 'deceptive speaking', the 'hunting' of people's hearts and minds) was to be located. Rashi quotes both of these views one after the other without further comment.

Again we need to go further behind this Rabbinic interpretation to understand it – there are always wheels within wheels. For the Rabbis, Jacob epitomized the people Israel, but Esau through a variety of transformations came to stand for Rome, the hated ruling power. Thus the attacks on Esau by the Rabbis are not merely arbitrary, but in a way represent a coded comment on their own contemporary times and problems. One has to remember that much of their 'midrash', when it was not dealing with legal matters, was actually homiletics, sermons addressed to their contemporaries. As Eveline Goodman-Thau pointed out in a previous chapter, if you wanted to find the answer, you had to look at the weekly reading from the Pentateuch and it would be there. Thus the Rabbis could read in the text their own interpretation of contemporary events, suitably disguised through the stories of the biblical characters. This possibility is even mentioned once or twice by the Rabbis (e.g. in Tanhuma, 3 *lekh lkha* 12). It was to be taken up by Nahmanides as a major exegetical principle (see his comment on Gen. 12.6) with the saying *ma'aseh avot siman l'banim*, 'the deeds of the fathers are signs to their children', thus the details of the lives and journeyings of the patriarchal are themselves full of contemporary meaning to those who are prepared to look carefully.

To return to Rashi, the word 'hunt' seems to him to be highly loaded, so that the combination of Nimrod's name and that word make him into a rebel against God and one who also led others astray. Incidentally Rashi breaks down the word 'before', as in 'before the Eternal' into its two components which would make it mean literally 'to the face', and thus has him provoking the Eternal 'to his face' in his second comment on the verse.

What does Ibn Ezra say? He begins:
Don't look for a meaning for all the names if it is not given explicitly.

This would appear to be a rejection of the interpretation of Nimrod's name as 'rebellion'. Why? Because elsewhere in the Bible where a name is given for a particular reason it is actually spelled out – thus Isaac's name means 'laughter' as the text in Genesis explains to us a number of times (Gen. 18.10–15; 21.1–7). Since there is no such indication here in the text that we are to understand the name as expressing some aspect of Nimrod's character, we are not entitled to read anything into it! So much for Rashi and the Rabbis. He continues:

He [Nimrod] began to show the power of human beings over animals for he was a 'mighty hunter'. And the meaning of 'before the Eternal' is that he built altars and offered to God the animals he had killed. And that is the plain meaning, though the midrash is somewhat different.

Here we see Ibn Ezra at his most clear and explicit, searching for the common sense meaning of the verse, even though, as he himself notes, the traditional understanding is somewhat different.

Enter Ramban, who begins by quoting Rashi in full, adding only 'and that was the view of our sages'. He would appear to be in agreement. He then continues:

> But Rabbi Abraham explained it in the opposite way, according to the plain meaning, that he began to act in a mighty way against the animals by hunting them. And he explained 'before the Eternal' to mean that he built altars to offer up the animals as an offering before God. But his [Ibn Ezra's] words are not acceptable (literally, do not appear), for he is actually justifying a wicked person, for our sages knew of his wickedness from tradition. So the correct understanding in my view is that he began to rule through his power over people and he was the first to become a king, for until his time there were no wars and no king ruled. First he overpowered the people of Babel until he ruled them, then he went out to Assyria and did as he wished and grew great and built there fortified cities through his power and might, and hence it says in the next verse: and the beginning of his kingdom was Babel . . .

What seems to scandalize Ramban is Ibn Ezra's cavalier treatment of the traditional view of Nimrod, and we have to understand and respect the enormous weight he would have placed upon Rabbinic interpretation. Perhaps it would be as fair to say that Ibn Ezra was equally scandalized by dependence on a tradition that flew in the face of rationality and common sense. But more than that, Ramban seems to feel the depiction of a real evil force at the heart of the description of Nimrod. To vindicate him, given the knowledge the Rabbis had handed down to us, may well have been unacceptable to his sense of justice. But note that for all his valuing of that same tradition, while he records the Rabbinic view as expressed by Rashi, he nevertheless feels the need to offer his own version of the 'plain meaning'. Perhaps he is influenced here by the other meaning of *gibbor* as 'warrior' and thus sees Nimrod as a conqueror, the inventor of wars and the creator of empire.

What Ibn Ezra might have said to counter-attack, or how Rashi might have attempted to mediate, cannot be known. It is for us to pick our hero and take up the cudgels on his behalf if we so wish.

For those who have enjoyed this brief taste of Rabbinic debate the best thing to do, short of mastering the subject yourself, is to read the commentaries of Professor Nechama Leibowitz listed below in the Further Reading section p. 179. She brings dozens of different commentators together on particular verses and has them argue with each other, at the same time demanding that we do not stand neutrally by but join in. Nahmanides disputation with Pablo Christiani is brilliantly presented by Hyam Maccoby – again see below for the details.

We have seen how the Rabbinic need to speak to their times, how Ibn Ezra's rational mind and Rashi's veneration for tradition will colour their own approach to the same passage. It is time to examine further the way in which our own particular interests affect the way we read.

5

How a Donkey Reads the Bible
– On Interpretation

I sometimes ask a Bible class, 'If you were a donkey, what would you look for when you read the Bible?' The answer comes quite readily, 'stories about donkeys'. And they are not hard to find. Abraham and Moses and Samuel had famous donkeys that they rode. (In donkey terms it is somewhat disappointing that you have to be named in relation to some human being and not in terms of your own pedigree, but there is little you can do about it.) Perhaps the most celebrated is Balaam's donkey, who was certainly more perceptive than his master and suffered because of it, only to triumph in the end. One would spend a lot of time in awed discussion of that saintly beast.

Incidentally the Rabbis, who shared something of the Bible's unease with miracles, added Balaam's donkey to Jonah's fish and a few other wonders that, according to them, were all created in the twilight period between the end of the six days of creation and the beginning of the Shabbat, so that they were already in existence and could be inserted on the appropriate occasion by God. They also thought that after this episode Balaam's donkey died – because God did not want people to point to it and remember how Balaam had been upstaged by it. In their eyes, to shame someone in public was equivalent to killing them, so better the donkey should die instead – another sacrifice the worthy beast made for humanity.

As donkeys ourselves, we would definitely spend some time complaining about the literary treatment given to Saul's donkeys whose absence set him off on the journey that would eventually lead to his becoming king. The text has the gall to suggest that the donkeys of Saul's father were 'lost'! From the anthropocentric view of the text their temporary absence might well be understood as being 'lost', but from the donkeys' point of view this was anything but the case. They might have been on holiday, touring, visiting friends, having an adventure, any of a number of options. It all depends on your perspective and it is about time donkeys had a say in the way they are depicted and their behaviour evaluated – forward donkey liberation!

While all the above may be going a bit over the top, the point I am trying to make is quite simple. When we read a text we bring to it an enormous number of presuppositions related to our experience, knowledge, personal situation, tradition etc. We are none of us objective readers of the text, we are only more or less conscious of the degree to which our reading is coloured by our particular circumstances and the *zeitgeist*, the spirit of the times in which we live.

I once had an argument with a professor of Bible in Israel who told me that she would not recommend a certain Bible commentary series to her students even though she used it herself and found it helpful. Why? Because the series was published by a strictly orthodox Jewish publishing house and there was a particular disclaimer in the front of the book that she found unacceptable. It said, in effect, that: 'we include all findings of modern scholarly research insofar as they do not contradict the views of rabbinic tradition.' (Given the freedom of thought that is such an intrinsic part of Jewish tradition, the attitude of today's Jewish 'fundamentalists' is singularly un-Jewish. It may even be that the disclaimer was there to protect the writer from accusations of heresy as much as it was meant to encourage the traditionally-minded to read it without anxiety.)

I could just about see the Professor's point, after all, in Israel in particular, the secular, academic world sees itself locked in a '*kulturkampf*' with Orthodox Judaism, with the latter gaining enormously in power in recent years. The subsuming of scholarly findings to traditional beliefs would be unacceptable in any democratic situation and Israel is proud of its democratic tradition of freedom of speech and thought. In such a polarized situation people tend to side with one side of the argument or the other and indeed to have a pretty jaundiced view of each other. The desire of the professor to preserve academic integrity – all knowledge must be accepted at its face value and not selected according to some external criterion – seems very tenable.

However, I pointed out that there was a missing dimension to the argument. At least the person writing the commentary had put his cards on the table, identified very clearly where he came from and the limitations it placed upon his scholarship. Given that knowledge, people were free to make use of his book as they wished, but at least they had some way of assessing the value of its contents for their own particular purposes. But if one turned to the professor, what were the presuppositions under which she worked, how far did her own demand for 'objective' scholarship, itself a highly loaded term, actually colour and indeed limit her own ability to read what is, after all, a 'sacred text'. Indeed it may be that as with so many 'secular people', there is either an antagonism to religion or discomfort in its presence that must inevitably distort their view of so 'loaded' a book as the Bible. Yet where was the professor's disclaimer or any evidence of her own self-evaluation.

I should add at once that the professor in question is a marvellous humanitarian person, and the book in question is remarkably open in its use of scholarship given its background – just to make sure that I do not myself create too many stereotypes in passing. The book uses an odd device whereby the more conventional comments on the biblical passages are written directly beneath the biblical text in simple modern Hebrew that is 'pointed', that is to say, the vowel signs are added for ease of reading. But there is a second apparatus, in smaller print beneath the first, unpointed, in which he brings a lot of the scholarly material, usually introduced as 'there are also some who say' without comment or even crediting the author – thus even a secular scholar might be smuggled through this backdoor into heaven.

Just to continue this theme of the 'politics' of scholarship, I recall a totally different conflict which came up at the time I was working on my PhD. Two scholars from the Literature Department of the University of Tel Aviv, Menachem Perry and Meir Sternberg, published a long, fascinating and provocative article in the University's literary magazine *Hasifrut* (Literature) in which they analysed the biblical story of King David's affair with Bathsheba (II Sam. 11). They showed that on first reading the chapter we feel that the author is taking a neutral, detached view of the events in question, neither condoning nor condemning David. Only at the end with the closing phrase, 'but the thing that David did was bad in the sight of the Eternal', did the author bring some judgment on David's behaviour. (This would suggest to other schools of exegesis that this 'moralistic judgment' was actually tacked on in the editorial process because it did not fit the 'neutral tone' of the rest of the chapter.) However, they went on to examine verse by verse the way the story was told and a deep underlying irony that they felt was present throughout.

If you recall the story, David is back in his palace while the army is at war – already a problematic issue in a king whose success was built on his military prowess and 'presence'. He overlooks Bathsheba bathing on her roof, takes her to his bed and she becomes pregnant. (The scholars noted how often in the story anonymous agents are being sent around the palace bringing information about and from Bathsheba, as well as messages to and from the front – David sits in the centre of a spider's web of intrigue, Camelot has turned into Versailles.) David sends for Uriah the Hittite, Bathsheba's husband, ostensibly to bring news about the war, but actually so that he will return home, sleep with his wife and provide a convenient father for the child. But Uriah refuses to go home despite being pressed on the point. In desperation David sends him back to the front carrying his own death warrant in a secret message to Joab David's general in the field to put Uriah in a place at the front of the battle, retreat from him, and thus get him killed. Joab does so and sends back a rather contrived reply to David. Bathsheba mourns Uriah and marries David. Happy end! 'But the thing that David did was bad in the sight of the Eternal'.

Perry and Sternberg noted among many other things the problem that David faced in trying to interpret Uriah's behaviour. Did he refuse to visit his wife because he knew what David had done and was not prepared to satisfy him, or was he, as he claimed, a simple, loyal soldier, not prepared to indulge in luxurious living, and indeed enjoy intercourse with his wife, while his comrades were dying at the front – which in itself is Uriah's or the biblical narrator's pointed comment at David's expense. What the author of the story has achieved is to provide a number of 'gaps' in the text whereby we the readers are forced to guess which of two possible explanations is there and build our own suppositions on that, to have them confirmed or confounded or left in the air as the story unfolds. Moreover in this respect we are in the identical position as David, desperately trying to read the situation till he has no choice other than to confess – or resort to violence.

The point the scholars are making is that rather than being a 'neutral' recounting of the tale, the author is writing highly critically and ironically at David's expense. Thus the closing 'judgment' from God is not an afterthought or editorial gloss, but the final ironic comment that seals the chapter.

When this article appeared there were two strong attacks on it from members of the Department of Bible Studies of the Universities of Tel Aviv and Bar Ilan. They questioned the validity of this approach in the first place as it ignored the critical problems of the composition of the text. They challenged what they considered the arbitrary decision of the two scholars to stop their analysis at the end of chapter 11 when the story continues into chapter 12. This contains the famous parable that the prophet Nathan brings to David, about the rich man who stole the favourite little lamb of his poor neighbour, so that David comes to condemn himself out of his own mouth, and all the subsequent tragedies that take place as the child of Bathsheba dies. Perry and Sternberg replied in a sixty page article (bearing in mind it was printed in very small Hebrew print you have to double it to translate it into English pages!) in which they attacked their critics for sticking to outmoded critical prejudices and generally gave as good as they got.

But for all the heat of the criticism and response, the two sides were not too far away from each other in their understanding of the story as a whole. Thus as much as this was a scholarly disagreement about the reading of a particular text, it was also a 'demarcation dispute' in which the biblical scholars were challenging the right of 'literature' scholars to muscle in on their turf. In fact it was one of the opening shots in a battle that has been fought for the last twenty years, particularly in America and England, with the 'literary scholars' having had an enormous success and helping to re-shape the whole contemporary scholarly approach to Bible. But the point I want to make here is to illustrate once more that we come to the text with a variety of 'traditions' behind us which colour our understanding in subtle, and sometimes highly 'political' ways.

To show how wide-ranging, and on a certain level, predictable, different approaches to the Bible may be, it is worth mentioning an interesting experiment we conducted one evening at the Jewish-Christian Bible Week in Bendorf. We usually start the first evening with a short 'game' that gets people into the study ahead of us, allows them to meet a few new faces, and gets them safely to bed relatively early after a long journey to reach the place. On this occasion I produced a translation of 'Au Claire de la Lune', insofar as my memory of the song and my ability with French were up to it. I distributed it to about ten groups, randomly chosen, with the explanation that this was a text found in a Mongolian settlement from about the second millennium BCE. Each group was given an identity as a particular named person or representative of a profession and had to interpret the text in their own terms, then read out their explanations at the end. They were to conceal their identity when explaining their findings which allowed the other groups to guess who or what they were. The text was as follows.

In the light of the moon
my friend Piro
lend me your pen
to write a word
my candle is dead
I have no more fire
open for me your door
for the love of God

The first group noted the scandalous situation that forced someone to work so long during the day that they had no time for their private lives until late at night, and that even then the basic necessities of life, including heat and light, were not available to them. In these circumstances they were thrown back on the panacea of seeking help from the love of God instead of identifying the true source of their servitude in the system itself and revolting against it.

The group was rightly identified by the others as representing a Marxist theoretician.

The second group apologized to the others for entering such uncomfortable areas but noted that the imagery of a dead candle with no more fire was clearly sexual. It drew attention to the archetypal significance of the moon and the importance of its appearance in dreams because it symbolized the desire for enlightenment, however there was also evidence of a block to further insight as represented by the closed door.

The 'psychotherapist' was quickly identified.

And so it went on with each of the groups. The reference to the moon, hence moon worship, and the description of the extinguished candle, suggested to 'Erich von Daniken' a folk memory of the arrival from another planet and the dying fires of the space ship. Conversely 'Werner Keller' found in the same reference to the moon in a Mongolian document from the second millennium a confirmation that the moon had already been created by that time exactly in accord with what was stated in Genesis chapter one.

By the end of the evening, the 'protestant Bible scholar', the 'liberation theologian', the 'feminist', the 'hasidic rebbe' and even the 'journalist', had all been identified without much difficulty by the groups. Which is only to acknowledge on one level a degree of

prejudice we all have about the positions of different people or
types, but also the extent to which such positions bring identifiably
different concerns to reading a text. In this case it was a 'neutral'
one, which gave us a useful perspective on our work the following
week with the Bible itself, which is eminently more loaded with
expectations and presuppositions.

Apropos the 'psychotherapist', I cannot resist adding a fascinating piece of exegesis of the Book of Jonah I came across while
researching my PhD. A psychoanalyst had made a study of the book
and came to the following conclusions.

The Book of Jonah was written following the serious illness or
death of the author's wife from a gynaecological disorder or as a
result of childbirth.

This breathtaking conclusion was explained as follows. The book
contains a lot of womb symbolism, most notably the 'great fish' that
swallowed Jonah, but also the 'gourd' in chapter 4 that shelters
Jonah from the sun. However the gourd is struck down by a worm,
which is clearly a phallic symbol. Thus the author was expressing his
guilt about damage caused to his wife, who on another level was
really his 'mother', as a consequence of sexual intercourse.

Before we dismiss this reading, it is important to recognize what is
actually going on here. The author has been translating one
symbolic language, that of the biblical narrative, into another, that
of a particular psychoanalytical world. The exercise is as legitimate
in its own terms as any other mode of interpretation that we
undertake. It is no less peculiar, in this sense, to derive a large part
of the Jewish dietary laws from a verse about 'not seething a kid in
its mother's milk' or the 'virgin birth' from the questionable
translation of the word for an 'unmarried girl' in Isaiah 7.14.
Beyond the legitimacy of any particular interpretation is the
question of whether one is consequent or not in the value system
one builds upon it.

The problem of the presuppositions we bring to the text were
already aired by the Rabbis, particularly as expressed in certain
debates between Rabbi Ishmael and Rabbi Akiba. Akiba was
famous for his valuing of every single letter of Torah as being filled
with significance and interpretative potential. This fits in well with
his reputation as a mystic, the Rabbi who 'rescued' the Song of
Songs from the local hostelries and saw it as the holiest of
expressions of divine love. Such was his commitment to Torah that

he continued to teach it in public despite a Roman ban and died as a
martyr at the hands of Roman torturers.

He is famous for one particular method of exegesis which brought
him into conflict with his colleague Ishmael. In the Hebrew Bible
are a number of 'particles', like for example the word *et* which has
no meaning but which stands before a particular word in a sentence
to indicate that it is the object of the preceding verb. 'In the
beginning God created *et* the heavens and *et* the earth.' This did not
satisfy Akiba who found in such words a source of enlarging the
content of what followed to include more than merely the word.
Conversely there are other particles that were seen as setting a
limitation on the particular law that contained them. Thus the
phrase in Exodus 31.13 '*but* you shall keep My sabbaths' contains
the particle '*akh*', (but). The presence of the 'but' is to indicate that
there may be occasions when the Sabbath may be broken. When?
When life would be endangered by keeping it – a principle that has
had considerable importance in Jewish life.

There is a story told about one of Akiba's pupils who tried to
emulate his master and went consistently through the Bible
explaining every single one of these particles on the basis of his
master's teaching – such students were no less a problem in those
days. He did very well until he reached the verse in Deuteronomy
10.20 'and you shall fear your God'. How could you fear something
more than God or other than God? At this point the student gave
up. His own pupils came to him and asked: 'How can you give up
now?' He replied: 'All the merit that I acquired for explaining all
these things will be matched by the merit I acquire for admitting I
was wrong.' There is intellectual honesty! Inevitably, Akiba was
less impressed and proceeded to explain the verse: Whom else do
you fear beside God, the teachers who bring you to the fear of God!

But Ishmael had to point out the excesses of some of Akiba's
interpretations, particularly where they had legal consequences. He
himself utilized thirteen hermeneutical principles, inherited largely
from the first-century teacher Hillel, for deriving legal decisions
from the existing laws in the Hebrew Bible. Thus for example if two
passages give contradictory views on a particular subject, the
solution can only be obtained by finding a third verse that resolves
the problem. Or the presence of the same word in two different
legal contexts allows one to compare the two contexts in deriving
new laws – though certain other rules applied limiting the words that
could be used for such a comparison. Thus, as indeed for Akiba, we

are dealing with the Bible as a closed universe but one which can be manipulated by the use of accepted exegetical principles.

Ishmael is the author of a statement that has enormous consequences on the way later Jewish exegetes were able to read the text, particularly the approach we have seen used by Ibn Ezra. He coined the phrase: '*dibra torah kilshon benei adam*' 'Torah speaks in human language'. One way of understanding that is precisely in opposition to Akiba: when God communicates with human beings through the medium of a language God too is bound by Hebrew grammar! Or to put it another way, one has also to take into account common sense in utilizing the biblical text.

Another Rabbinic saying that has important consequences for later Jewish interpretations is, *ayn mukdam ume'uhar batorah*, literally, 'there is no before and after in the Torah'. That is to say that the sequence of events described in the biblical narratives may not be given in chronological order. This is a remarkable principle, as it is effectively a way of stepping back from the text and acknowledging that it has been 'edited' so that passages may be linked by other than the apparent chronological sequence.

Another Rabbinic view is that 'no two prophets prophesy in the same style', a recognition that the message of the prophets is affected by their own personal circumstances, qualities and indeed literary abilities. These observations and indeed the vast amount of exegetical material that explores the biblical text in the pages of the Talmud and Midrash, serve to remind us that the problem of *who* is reading the text has been with us for as long as the problem of *what* we read in the text.

I would like to pull these various ideas together by looking at a particular text whose interpretation is coloured by its actual location within the Hebrew Bible. However, the specific interpretation that I will give to it is very much the product of the experience of the twentieth century.

There is a 'built-in' ordering of the biblical books that makes for a major difference in perception between Jews and Christians. The second major division of the Hebrew Bible, the prophets, runs from the Book of Joshua to the end of the twelve 'minor prophets'. It includes, in order, Joshua, Judges, I and II Samuel, I and II Kings, Isaiah, Jeremiah, Ezekiel and the 'Twelve'. Joshua to the end of Kings are the 'Former Prophets', Isaiah to the end of the 'Twelve', the 'Latter Prophets'. However in the King James version, inserted within the section of 'Former Prophets' are also the Book of Ruth (following Judges), Ezra, Nehemiah and I and II Chronicles. That is to say the ordering seems to be based on seeing these volumes as 'historical', recounting the story of the conquest, the monarchy, the destruction of the two kingdoms and the return from Babylon. Since they are the identical books, does the change of sequence matter?

Let us look at a story in the Book of Judges and see what difference it makes whether we read it as 'history' or 'prophecy'.

In Judges 9 occurs the story of Abimelech. We are introduced to him in the previous chapter:

> Gideon had seventy sons who came out from his loins for he had many wives. Moreover, his concubine who was in Shechem also bore him a son, and he called his name Abimelech. (Judg. 8.30–31)

The fact that Abimelech's mother came from Shechem, and her status as concubine, would suggest that she did not belong to one of the Israelite tribes but to the local Canaanite community, which would seem to be borne out by the association of her family with the Baal worship in the area.

Before reading the story we need to have two more pieces of information. Gideon, one of the 'judges' who arose to save Israel from their enemies, following the pattern of stories in the Book of Judges, was also known as Jerubaal, because he had smashed the altar of 'Baal'. He was offered the opportunity to create a dynastic rule over the tribes of Israel but turned it down:

> The men of Israel said to Gideon: 'Rule over us, you and your sons and your sons' sons, for you have saved us from the hands of Midian.' But Gideon said to them: 'I will not rule over you, nor will my son rule over you, the Eternal will rule over you.' (Judg. 8.22–23)

This raises an interesting question about the naming of Abimelech, which means 'My father is king'. Given Gideon's reluctance to rule, and Abimelech's attempt to become king, it is interesting to guess who actually gave him that name. The text is not fully clear, though the obvious subject is Gideon, which might mean that he was less reluctant to accept the title than he had suggested or was behaving whimsically in giving the name to this son of the outsider. Or it might have been the name Abimelech took for himself once his ambition had been reached.

The story itself is brief and violent:

> Abimelech the son of Jerubaal went to Shechem to the brothers of his mother and spoke to them and to all the family of the house of his mother's father, saying: Please speak in the ears of all the prominent citizens of Shechem, [asking] 'which is better for you – that seventy men rule over you, all the sons of Jerubaal, or that one man rule over you? And remember that I am your flesh and blood.'
>
> So the brothers of his mother spoke all these things on his behalf in the ears of all the prominent citizens of Shechem and turned their hearts after Abimelech, for they said: 'He is our brother!' Then they gave him seventy [pieces] of silver from the house of Baal-Brit and with them Abimelech hired men, empty and undisciplined, and they followed him. He came to the house of his father at Ephrat and killed his brothers, the sons of Jerubaal, seventy men upon a single stone, and only Jotham the youngest son of Jerubaal survived because he was hidden.
>
> Then all the prominent citizens of Shechem and of Beth Milo gathered and went and crowned Abimelech as king at Alon Mutzav which is in Shechem. (Judg. 9.1–6)

The stages of Abimelech's rise to power are easy to plot. He turns to his mother's family, presumably playing on the tensions between the two local communities and the power that now lies in the hands of Gideon's sons. He asks them to speak to the *baaley shechem*, literally the 'masters of Shechem', the same term '*baal* being used for the Canaanite deities. Presumably it means here those with authority and power within Shechem. He raises two questions. The first is open to a variety of interpretations, but it is very easy to find in it a contemporary ring. That the seventy sons of Jerubaal rule suggests merely the nepotism that is the norm in a tribal society. But the contrast with the 'one' ruler suggests other questions about the power and authority of leadership, the effectiveness or otherwise of a plurality of rulers, in our own terms democracy versus autocracy. However it is seen in detail, Abimelech dresses his political ambitions in the language of local needs. But his second point is ultimately more persuasive – the appeal to their own self-interest – 'and remember, I am your flesh and blood'. And indeed it is to that

that they respond and agree to support him 'because they said, "He is our brother."'

Any political campaign, or revolution, needs funding so they go to the house of the Baal of the Covenant (*Baal brit*), presumably the Temple of their local deity. With this money Abimelech recruits an army from the local riff-raff. The terms 'empty and undisciplined' would suggest people without a stake in the society, unattached formally to any families in the local community and probably living as outlaws. Thus armed with his little band of mercenaries, Abimelech goes and murders his brothers. What distinguishes this act from a mere massacre is the unusual phrase 'on a single stone', the meaning of which is unclear. It will have an echo later in the story when, measure for measure, Abimelech is mortally wounded by a millstone that is thrown on to his head by a woman while he is besieging Tebetz. But what does it mean here? Bearing in mind the degree to which Abimelech has played the game so far along fairly well trodden political lines, gaining a constituency, formal financial support from the leaders of the community and incidentally the local 'church', it may be that even this act was given the air of spurious legitimacy. For this might suggest a formal execution, one by one at the place of execution, of the seventy sons of Jerubaal, perhaps even following a trial of some sort in which their various failings and abuses of power were put on display. At this point I acknowledge that I am going beyond the evidence, but the riddle of the single stone remains to be resolved.

Finally, despite Abimelech's actions, or even because of them, the leaders of Shechem appoint him as king – which ushers in Abimelech's bloody reign till he too is killed.

Why bring this particular story – or as it was once formulated, what's a nasty story like this doing in a nice book like the Bible? When I first read it with some degree of attention, the parallels to the rise of Hitler, or for that matter any demagogue, struck me very forcibly. The political stages of appealing to the self-interest of a threatened or disenfranchised power elite; the alliance between them and the church; the creation of a private army from the underworld; the use of pseudo-legality when it suited the purpose, combined with utter ruthlessness and murder. Finally the gaining of authority even though those who bestowed it knew what the new leader was capable of doing – for which incidentally the people of Shechem are condemned at the end of the chapter (9.56–57).

All of the above make this story not merely a piece of ancient history, but 'prophetic' in that precise sense of viewing human actions from a divine perspective, of recognizing the implications of certain patterns of behaviour as they actually develop, and warning against them. Prophecy in this biblical sense is always conditional upon human responses, the prophet merely clarifies the reality and the options and warns.

In these terms it makes an enormous difference whether we read the stories in the section from Joshua to the end of Kings as 'history' or as 'prophecy'. Are they ancient stories from the pre-history of Israel that are of passing interest only, or are they in some sense archetypal tales about human actions that serve as warnings and challenges to subsequent generations? Indeed of all the materials of its early history that was available to the compilers of these books why were these particular episodes selected? The answer of the Hebrew Bible in terms of the actual ordering of the books is that they are to be read as 'prophecy', though I hope I do not have to add that I do not believe that they 'prophesied the rise of Hitler' in some simplistic way. The world has seen too many Abimelechs.

'What's a nasty story like this doing in a nice book like the Bible?' First we should recognize what is actually in the Bible before we decide what kind of 'book' or 'library' it is. If donkeys only see stories about donkeys, perhaps nice people only see 'nice' things in the Bible. Somehow if we are to take the Bible seriously in its own terms, we do need to acknowledge time and time again the limitations our own background sets upon our ability to read it, and learn to share the perspectives and understandings of past and present 'readers' alike. To re-read Rabbi Ishmael, 'Torah speaks in the language and to the reality of human beings'.

6

My Part in the Fall of 'King David' – The Bible Goes to the Movies

The 'call' when it came, came not from God, at least not directly, but from Pinewood film studios. I was standing by the switchboard at Leo Baeck College. Some film company was looking for an expert on Bible, could we help? Without a moment's hesitation I modestly put myself forward. (Since two of my colleagues had already been advisers respectively on Zefferelli's 'Jesus of Nazareth' and Barbra Streisand's 'Yentl', I figured it was my turn.) Thus I became the technical adviser on 'King David', the first attempt in years at a major biblical epic. It took three months to film at a cost of thirty million dollars. It closed within a week in Los Angeles, but you can still get the video.

Slow fade.

Scene two, a cluttered office in Pinewood.

'The producer likes you!' He said this with the air of one who knows the whims of the gods and the importance of those they favour. The producer *should* like me! Apart from any personal qualities and abilities, it seems I was the first 'expert' willing to risk his reputation on the film. Jewish lobbies in America thought it was 'antisemitic' – because it was trying to depict King David 'as he really was'. It seemed a dubious argument. More to the point, the real scholars were shocked by the liberties taken by the script – and they had only seen the first of more than a score of drafts. But, what the hell, artistic licence and all that. Who could resist the lure of the cinema?

The director wanted to have someone on set throughout the shooting to advise on matters biblical. I was given some time off to join the company, and booked a colleague to be there when I could not make it. Sardinia, Matera, Rome, ah, the glamour.

Of course it is mostly hanging around and waiting. The film hit a lot of problems. It had been planned to shoot it in Morocco, but rumour had it that this was scotched when they found out that King David was Jewish. Israel had too many television aerials which got in the way of the long shots. Finally Southern Italy was chosen and a fibre glass replica of Jerusalem was built in Matera, where Pasolini had shot his 'The Gospel According to St Matthew'. It turned out to be the coldest spring in that part of the world for forty years so half the time was spent waiting for consistent weather conditions – it seems you cannot shoot half the scene in bright sunshine and the other half overcast. People notice such things, though rain apparently does not show up. I still enjoy the picture of the star, Richard Gere, sitting on a horse, about to leave the land of Israel to live among the Philistines, and intoning solemnly: 'Is not the heat of God's sun as great on the other side?' while trying to stop his teeth chattering.

For tax reasons, they started shooting in Pinewood before shipping out to Italy and used both British and Italian crews throughout – a source of entertaining cross-cultural conflict. (The British worked an hourly rate; the Italian unions insisted that everyone, and their entire families, be booked for the duration of the film, with consequent jealousies.) 'Saul's fortress' got adorned with a Union Jack when England beat Italy at a football game during the filming.

It did not take long to realize the problems that would beset a 'technical adviser'. We began at Pinewood with a banquet – David's marriage to Bathsheba. The extras, many of them elderly Jewish performers, did not seem to be enjoying the cold lamb chops that were meant to be the main course. So the director sent out to the local Chinese takeaway for spare ribs. My colleague, on duty at the time, tried to point out that pork spare ribs were not exactly permitted in biblical times, but was reassured that no one would notice.

However, he was to have his own moment of quiet triumph. Comes David's marriage to Michal, Saul's daughter, and they erected a *huppah*, the wedding canopy used in Jewish marriages. I objected that they never used them in Bible times but was overruled. 'We researched it', said the director. What research? They found a picture of a seventeenth-century Jewish wedding where they had a *huppah*, so they *must* have used them in the Bible. (I got used to that argument after a few times, though I never quite figured out when Australian Director Bruce Beresford had his tongue in his cheek.)

But the props man came up with a problem. 'It says in the script that there have to be wedding gifts on the set. What would they have been?' My colleague smiled to himself, gave him the appropriate information, saw out his time and returned to London. I took his place for the wedding scene itself – in fact I appear in the film reciting the Priestly Blessing over the couple. (It may not be worth watching the rest of the film just for those few moments, but you can always use the fast forward.) I arrived on the set to find a large box under the *huppah*. 'What's that for?' 'The wedding presents!' In fact it was a brilliant solution to the problem my colleague had presented to them – how do you show David's contribution of two hundred Philistine foreskins?

Actually, there was another foreskin involved in the film – it was, after all, meant to be authentic. The story called for a scene showing the circumcision of David's son Absolom. The shooting script had something like:

Shot of Nathan the prophet holding the knife.
Shot of a hand raised in the air and descending.
A splash of blood hits the screen.

I pointed out that if a splash of blood hit the screen they must have cut an artery by mistake, and goodbye Absolom. This script they changed.

I added a couple of authentic touches to this scene. (It got to be very frustrating being a 'technical adviser' whose advice, technical or otherwise, was almost never sought.) A couple of children are seen at the ceremony, pushing their way between the men and peeping at the goings on. That was my touch. Artistic.

I also proved my authority as an adviser here as well. I showed Richard Gere how to hold the baby (a good six months too old for the part!). You have to keep the legs apart with the knees bent so that the *mohel* (circumcisor) has a clear access. But I warned about one little snag that can happen at the best regulated circumcision. When the legs are pressed apart, the child may sometimes start to pee. And sure enough a golden fountain rose into the sky at the first rehearsal. My reputation was made!

Between weddings and circumcisions, I got to invent more biblical ceremonies than even Moses. But the most taxing was sacrificing a sheep on the altar in front of 'Jesse's farm'.

The altar was remarkable and 'authentic', an exact reproduction of an early Hittite one, said the art department. I was very impressed but had to point out that they had put it in the wrong place, in a little valley just in front of the house. 'Altars were put on the "high places"', I pointed out. The art director was adamant that this was the best location for the shot. The director appeased me in his usual reasonable manner: 'The ancient Israelites must have been practical people as well, and this was clearly the best place to put it.' I still do not know when he was being ironic at my expense and when at the expense of the film. Meeting him was one of the bonuses of the job.

The local vet turned up with a dopey (indeed doped) lamb for the dramatic shot where its neck would be cut. (Fear not, gentle reader, they use the remarkable concoction called in the trade 'Kensington Gore'. It consists of two liquids, each colourless, that produce a red colour when mixed – hence all those knives passing over the skin and producing a blooded cut in your average horror movie.)

There was much discussion about how exactly to do the throat slitting. If you ever see the film you will notice that the writer had a penchant for beheading people, so why not the odd sheep. (Goliath's decapitation is strictly biblical in origin, all the rest in the film are his own invention. Ponder the implications.)

I couldn't resist asking: 'Are you going to burn the sheep on the altar?'

'What do you mean?'

'Well, that's why they sacrificed the animal, to burn it on the altar – sometimes completely, sometimes as part of a common meal.'

'Nobody told us that! Why didn't you mention it yesterday? It's too late!'

But the director liked it. It added that touch of authenticity he wanted. That was why he had a technical adviser on the set.

The props man raised a small problem. The authentic Hittite altar was actually made of fibre glass – if you burnt anything on it it would go straight through.

The director was adamant.

The props man came up with an asbestos sheet which he laid on top of the altar and held down with some stones.

But what were we going to burn? The sheep was asleep by now and the vet looked nervous. The prop man sent an assistant to town to buy a bucket of sheep entrails, which were eventually smeared (I can think of no better word) on top of the altar. Now came the time to ignite them.

Sheep entrails do not burn.

On came an assistant prop man with paraffin, poured it over them and set them alight.

If you looked very closely, say from about two feet away, you could just about see a slight blue flame hovering over them. Not very convincing.

In the film itself there is a long shot of Samuel anointing the young David as the future king. In the background stands a magnificent, authentic Hittite altar with black smoke rising from it.

What you cannot see is a prop man crouched down behind the back of it with a smoke cannister sending up little puffs into the air.

It works, and that seems to be what matters in a film. The tricks and props and improvisations and fakery all disappear. It is quite disillusioning and in a perverse way very satisfying to know how the trick is pulled off. Working behind the scenes ruined the cinema for me for a long time afterwards. I found myself looking out for editorial cuts, camera tricks, fibre glass boulders, the familiar half-a-dozen fighting moves I'd seen the stuntmen practising. But the power of the cinema comes back on another level – the film fails if you find yourself more interested in the technique than in the content. That became a lasting lesson.

There is a similar danger with *tenakh*. The more you begin to look behind it to the construction of the plot, the way certain literary or poetic 'moves' are made, the rhetorical structures and the way the writer uses or subverts them, the more distanced you become for a while from the impact of the text itself.

Nevertheless, the cinema is one of the media that can actually cast a light on some of the effects of biblical narrative. Let us look at a few examples.

We are all used to slow motion. At some important event in the film, time is stretched out for us to an unbearable extent by running everything at a slower speed, delaying the climactic moment. The identical technique can be seen at work in the story of the 'Binding of Isaac', Genesis chapter 22. The three days journey that Abraham has to undertake is glossed over with a few words, but the act of preparing to kill his son is spelled out in incredible detail, each verb being literally stretched out to hold the suspense even longer.

They came to the place of which God had told him and there
Abraham built an altar
and he laid out the wood
and he bound his son
and he placed him upon the altar above the wood
and Abraham stretched out his hand
and he took the knife to slay his son.

Then called to him a messenger of the Eternal from heaven,
saying: 'Abraham, Abraham!' He said: 'Here I am!'

We are with Abraham in every detail and at every moment up to
the very last second when the voice comes to prevent him. The
writing itself suspends time.

In contrast we have at least one scene where the action is 'speeded
up' in true Keystone Cops style. In fact the very brevity of the
writing – a whole row of verbs strung together – indicates precisely
the character of the person being described, Esau, Jacob's brother.

When Esau returns from the field hungry, Jacob offers him some
food in exchange for this birthright. Look at the way the text
describes what happens:

> Jacob gave Esau bread and a bowl of soup –
> and he ate,
> drank,
> arose,
> went,
> despised his birthright. (Gen. 25.34)

The conventional translations have to insert 'and Esau despised',
but the series of verbs ends with that one before the name 'Esau'
reappears in the text. In fact the staccato effect is even clearer in the
Hebrew: '*vayokhal vayesht vayakom vayelekh vayivez*'.

There is a shocking scene in Peckinpah's 'The Wild Bunch', when
a gang of bandits are gunned down in the street. The scene is
particularly effective because it is not only played out in slow
motion, but a number of the passages of people and horses falling to
the ground are repeated over and over again. The technique has
been used many times since (notably in the final death scene in
'Bonnie and Clyde') and for all I know has precedents in the
cinema, but the identical technique can be found in the 'Song of
Deborah' (Judg. 5.27) which describes the death of Sisera slain with
a tent-peg by Jael. Again, the Hebrew repetitions, because of their
very conciseness, are more powerful than the usual translations.

> *beyn ragleha kara nafal shakhav*
> *beyn ragleha kara nafal*
> *ka'asher kara sham nafal*
> *shadood.*
> Between her legs he bent, he fell, he lay
> between her legs he bent, he fell

where he bent there he fell,
shattered!

The above imagery is ambiguous. Sisera falling between the legs of Jael could carry a sexual connotation – how else was she able to get the better of him. Or, in a poem that will subsequently stress the tragedy of his mother waiting in vain for his return, it might also convey the image of a stillbirth, falling between the legs of its mother. However, since sexuality is never far from the box office, perhaps we should look at something in that area as well.

Before there was 'Rashomon' there was Mrs Potiphar. We have already seen Joseph's heroic refusal to succumb to her charms, but we did not look at the sequel. If you recall 'Rashomon', the film hinged around the way a variety of different people recall the same event from their own perspective. Each time it is utterly different which makes it a masterly study of the problem of witnessing, and indeed of interpreting things as well. The reason for raising it here is that it was 'prefigured' by Mrs Potiphar who tried more actively to seduce Joseph and he had to escape leaving some incriminating garments behind. As in 'Rashomon' we are treated to three versions of what happened, the narrator's view, Mrs Potiphar's version for the servants and a second version for her husband. See if you can spot not only the differences but also how she is actually attempting to manipulate the situation with the different 'facts' she establishes:

On that particular day when he [Joseph] came to the house to do his work, there was no one of the men of the house there in the house. And she grabbed him by his garment, saying, 'Lie with me!' and he left his garment in her hand and fled and went outside.

When she saw that he had left his garment in her hand and had fled outside, she called to the men of her house and said to them as follows: 'See, he has brought a Hebrew man to us to mock/seduce us. He came to me to sleep with me and I called out at the top of my voice! Then when he heard me raise my voice and call, he left his garment beside me and fled and went outside.'

And she kept his garment beside her until her husband came to his house. And she said to him the following sort of thing, saying: 'That Hebrew slave whom you brought to us came to me to seduce me! But when I raised my voice and I called out he left his garment near me and fled outside.' (Gen. 39.11–18)

It is an interesting exercise to see how many differences you can spot and why they were necessary. But did her husband believe her? Clearly Joseph was punished with imprisonment, though one suspects that the attempted rape of his master's wife would have deserved nothing less than the death penalty. It all depends on how you read the description of Potiphar's response, which is incidentally yet a fourth version of what happened. See what you think:

> When her husband heard the words of his wife which she said to him saying, 'these sorts of things your servant did to me', he was very angry (Gen. 39.19).

But with whom?

One technique that I presume we think of as unique to the cinema is the possibility of running a film backwards. I enjoy watching demolished buildings or chimney stacks returning to their former state. I carry in my head a memory of some figure in a Cocteau film rising mysteriously to his feet in an impossible way, only because the film has been reversed. But one particular image belongs to 'The Thief of Baghdad' – the genie in the lamp trick. Rubbing the lamp produced a cloud of smoke that rose into the air like an inverted pyramid and out of it emerged the genie – that at least is my memory. But even more effective was the reversal of the process so that the pyramid of smoke became 'sucked' back into the lamp as the genie returned. There is a strange, and indeed disturbing, prefiguration of that technique in a passage in the Book of Jeremiah. I will give the Hebrew in transliteration first so that two of the effects, the repetitions and the gradual shortening of the sentences may be more apparent:

> *raiti et-haaretz v'hiney tohu vavohu v'el hashamayim v'eyn oram*
> *raiti heharim v'hiney roashim v'khol hagvaot hitkalkalu*
> *raiti v'hiney eyn ha'adam v'khol off hashamayim nadadu*
> *raiti v'hiney hakarmel hamidbar v'khol arav nitzu*
> *mipney adonay*
> *mipney haron apo*

I looked at the earth and behold, empty and void; to the heavens, their light was no more.
I looked to the mountains and behold they shook and all the hills were quaking.
I looked and behold, no human being and all birds of the heavens had flown.

I looked and behold the pasture was desert and all its cities
destroyed,
because of the Eternal,
because of the heat of his anger. (Jer. 4.23–26)

Jeremiah depicts the end of the world, the return to primal chaos
– using the actual language of the first chapter of Genesis and
turning back the stages of creation. But not only that, he does it by
making each sentence shorter than the previous one, by repeating
certain words but gradually cutting whatever is inessential. When
the Hebrew is laid out it looks like an inverted triangle or a funnel as
indeed the world shrinks back in on itself to disappear into the anger
of God. The imagination of a Jeremiah can conceive and depict
something that we are only just beginning to recognize in our age of
potential nuclear destruction.

Perhaps one of the most time-honoured clichés of the cinema is
the shot of a telephone, either in close-up or at the front of the
screen so that you see the other characters behind it. You know that
it is only a matter of time before it rings. The biblical equivalent of
that is the use of certain 'key words' whose repetition at crucial
moments establishes an underlying continuity between certain
events or passages. Few are as dramatic as the about-to-ring phone.
Instead they may serve as a linking image that prepares us in a quiet
way for a crucial moment, or, as in the case we will now examine,
also allows us to get a sense of passing time.

The particular image here is a cloak, Hebrew *me'il*. When the
childless Hannah prays at the sanctuary of Shiloh for a child, she
promises to dedicate it to God. She is granted her prayer and the
child Samuel is dedicated to the Temple and lives there with the
Priest Eli. The narrative conveys both the pain of her separation
from the child and her love for him by a simple device. 'A little cloak
his mother made for him and brought it to him from year to year
(literally "from days to days" – perhaps to emphasize how she
counted them) with her husband when she came to make the annual
sacrifice.' (I Sam. 2.19)

The cloak has been 'planted' and subconsciously we wait for its
reappearance. Meanwhile in the same chapter another device is
operating. There is always a problem for a narrative to depict
simultaneous events because it is literally impossible to write two
things on the same page – unless you use parallel columns. In effect
that is done by the cinema with a split screen, which allows you to

watch two simultaneous events, or at least try to, often moving on a collision course with each other. This chapter is constructed by switching between two parallel scenes to create much the same effect. Thus it devotes one verse to the arrival of Samuel at Shiloh (v. 11), then spends the next six verses depicting very graphically the particular crimes of Eli's sons as they misuse their power (vv. 12–17). Then we switch back to the annual visit of Hannah and her husband and Samuel's growth (vv. 18–21). With that established, it is back to Eli remonstrating his sons on their behaviour and their refusal to listen (vv. 22–25). Back again to Samuel, now a lad growing in size and favour with God and the people (v. 24). Back to Eli and the arrival of a prophet who spells out the punishment to come upon his family for the sins of his sons (vv. 27–36). Chapter 3 shows us once again the lad Samuel serving God before Eli, as a prelude to the famous call he will receive in the middle of the night. This 'split screen' has allowed us to see the activities of the sons of Eli, his failure to correct them and the threat of punishment to come – while on the parallel screen in significant contrast Samuel grows up, acting properly in the service of God. While the scenes with Eli and his family are somehow crowded and busy, the quiet repetition of the same few phrases about Samuel and his single presence 'on the screen' give him a kind of composure and calm. That the two sides of the screen must meet in conflict is also clear, and indeed Samuel will bring the final warning to Eli and ultimately replace him as Priest at Shiloh – though ironically his own sons will behave no better than Eli's.

But all of that is in the future, and far in the future is the reappearance of the 'cloak'.

We meet it again, or rather perhaps we do, at a crucial moment in the tragic history of King Saul in his relationship with Samuel. Samuel has been ambiguous from the beginning about giving the people a king, and Saul, for all his magnificent stature, has shown himself to be weak, at least in Samuel's view. The reader is constantly torn between his sense of loyalty to one or other of the characters in these powerful stories. In chapter 15 the clash between Saul and Samuel reaches its climax, Saul fails to massacre the Amalekites as God has commanded and Samuel tells him that God has rejected him as King over Israel.

Samuel turned to go and he caught hold of the corner of his cloak and it tore. Samuel said to him, 'The Eternal has torn the kingship of Israel from you this day and given it to your neighbour who is better than you. (I Sam. 15.27–28)

The cloak is again the same word, but the text is disturbingly ambiguous. Did Samuel tear Saul's cloak from him as a symbolic gesture of the loss of his power? Or did Saul grasp Samuel's 'famous' cloak to make him stay and as if to mark the permanent rift between them, found it tearing apart in his hand? Whose cloak? It could be either, because a few chapters later David will cut off the corner of Saul's cloak (the same word) to show how he could have taken his life – but thereby ironically repeating the symbolic gesture of taking away his kingdom (I Sam. 24.5). But there is yet one more appearance of a cloak, and this time it is definitely Samuel's. When Saul is about to fight his final battle and has received no help from the normal prophetic channels to God, he resorts to necromancy, something he has himself banned from the country. He finds the witch of Endor and asks her to conjure up Samuel:

The woman saw Samuel and let out a great shriek, and said to Saul: 'Why did you deceive me? You are Saul!'
But the king said: 'Do not fear. What have you seen?'
The woman said to Saul: 'I have seen a great figure arising out of the earth.'
He said to her: 'What is his appearance?'
She said: 'An old man is rising up and he is wrapped in a cloak.'
And Saul knew that it was Samuel and he bent his face to the ground and bowed.

It is not clear whether this scene is meant to be played out in reality or in Saul's fantasy; whether the news that Samuel brings of his inevitable defeat is a final message from the prophet or Saul's inner acknowledgment that his end has come. It is a most powerful and moving story. And there in the centre, the symbol of recognition that also holds together the entire story of Samuel and his relationship with Saul is the 'cloak'.

We have somehow returned to the other 'King David' – and indeed Edward Woodward made a bravura attempt at Saul. It is the powerful effect of the cinema to play out before our eyes the things of fantasy. The Bible could work on the same level, but had to do it through words and sounds alone and a whole repertoire of devices, devices that probably worked more effectively for a community used to listening to the recital of events rather than reading them for themselves – and certainly not seeing them with all the sophisticated techniques of the contemporary cinema.

As a film, 'King David' was a box-office failure, but despite a lot of flaws, it was a courageous attempt to enter the biblical world. The result was somewhere between Cecil B. DeMille and a spaghetti western. But it took risks. King David danced before the ark, a very difficult scene to sustain and one which no previous film had even attempted. Richard Gere had to unlearn disco dancing for the scene and did make a remarkably powerful attempt. Presumably Gere was cast for his box office power, so he seemed a bit out of place among the rest of the cast – a method actor among British or British-style thespians. While King Saul was doing a replay of Lear, David was looking for his connection.

But these are minor problems. The film stands or falls by the script's reading of David, and it is probably here that it came most unstuck. The writer tried to make him a pacifist, tragically called upon to enter the arena of war instead of staying home and writing the Psalms. On beheading Goliath he looks sorrowfully to heaven and asks if that was really the only way to solve problems. It is a view of David, but does not really square with the figure depicted in the Books of Samuel who is nothing if not ruthless, while at the same time, through a certain charm, leaving the reader puzzled about the degree of his complicity in any number of misdeeds. He is deeply religious but expresses this in terms of his own time veering between fanatical enthusiasm for God and pragmatic utilization of religious symbols to strengthen his grip on the kingdom. We cannot get through the many faces of the biblical David to a single clear image, which is exactly the power of the biblical narrative. And the same must be said for Saul and Samuel who also become rather caricatured in the film, especially Samuel as the vengeful voice of a violent and angry God. In fact there is just a little too much of the stereotyped violent 'Old Testament' in this crucial area of the writing of the film.

But my point is not just to complain and hint that I could have done better. The film failed most when it left the biblical text and tried to invent sub-plots and condense separate events. That text is still awaiting serious artistic translation into the medium of film. Rather, for all its failures, it was important to have a go, if only to offer yet another attempt to get to grips with the Bible from a whole new range of presuppositions, viewpoints and intentions. The fact of filming means that things we might otherwise take for granted have actually to be visualized and indeed interpreted. Thus new tools are brought to bear and inevitably new insights obtained, however remote they may be from the customary forum of Bible study. But the Bible has always been too important a book to be left in the hands of the pious alone.

Like art itself, religion seems to depend on how far we are prepared to take risks.

7

Risking – The Bible
and Creativity

Occasionally I play a little harmonica. Once you get the hang of when to use your tongue to block the holes, and how to blow and suck without asphyxiating yourself, it is a marvellous instrument to carry around. But I wanted to play the blues. In particular to create that strange wailing sound that was all the rage in the blues revival of the sixties. So I bought a 'blues harmonica', one with chords built in instead of a straight scale, and blew it. I couldn't get the sound. So I went to a music shop in Charing Cross Road and asked the man behind the counter if there was a beginner's manual for learning to play the blues. The answer I got, from a customer next to me, was pretty much inevitable. 'You don't *learn* the blues, man,' he said, 'you *feel* it!' I left suitably demolished.

He was right, but he was also wrong. There is a technique you have to know before you can do anything else. (For those who want to try it I can only tell you that to play in the scale of E you have to use an A harmonica. The extra pressure you put on the reeds to bring the notes down to the right place produces the wail. Now all you have to do is *feel* it.)

So you need to know the technique, have a little native ability and off you go. But the next step is harder, the transforming of these skills and gifts into something that is art. Presumably the same factors apply whatever the medium, but I actually heard the following from an interview on the radio with a black jazz musician, talking about improvisation. 'I kind of get myself lost,' he said, 'and then I have to find my way back again.' And that's all there is to it. Great art, and perhaps also great religion, is 'risking'.

I continue to be astonished by the breathtaking courage of the author of the Book of Jonah, for one sentence in particular. It comes in chapter 4, after all Jonah's adventures in the fish and his successful impact on the people of Nineveh, to his own considerable anger. Impatient and intolerant he stands before God in prayer and lets off steam. To appreciate the passage we need to look at a few parts of it in isolation.

He starts (Jonah 4.2) with the opening prayer formula 'Please, O Eternal . . .', the identical formula used by the sailors in chapter 1 (v. 14) when they pray to God in fear of their lives. A good 'form critic', one concerned with the formal phrases and structures of certain types of rhetoric, would note this similarity and identify here a typical way of addressing God. The sailors then make their request, using another word for 'please' and a verb. Jonah does likewise, but we have to wait to the end of his very long statement (it lasts for two verses) to hear it: 'Please take my life from me for my death is better than my life.'

But in between these two formal pieces, something else breaks through, Jonah's pent up frustration and anger. Between the hands piously clasped in prayer, or possibly held up to heaven, there bursts out: 'Isn't this just what I said when I was back home!' That is the first shock, the shattering of the almost begging implications of the opening formula of prayer. But there is worse to come.

When Moses stood at Mount Sinai and pleaded for the life of his people after the episode with the Golden Calf, he asked God to show him the divine qualities. God answers with a remarkable passage listing them (Ex. 34.6–7):

The Eternal, the Eternal, God loving and gracious, long-suffering and great in faithful love and truth, keeping this faithful love for a thousand generations, forgiving iniquity, rebellion and failure, but not proclaiming the guilty innocent, visiting the sins of the fathers upon all their contemporary generations, sons, son's sons to the third and fourth generation.

It is worth noting that in this translation I follow Martin Buber's view that the phrase 'third and fourth generation' does not mean that sins continue to be visited into generations yet unborn, something completely a variance with the views of divine justice presented throughout the Hebrew Bible. Rather it is a warning that all generations alive at the time (great-grandfather, grandfather, father and son) are affected by and thus bear responsibility for the wrongs committed by the paterfamilias. The contrast is thus effectively made between 'a thousand generations' and 'one generation'.

What matters with regard to Jonah, is that this passage was clearly so central in the minds of the authors and compilers of the Hebrew Bible that it recurs with variations in a number of places, each time with a different nuance. Moses tosses it back to God on another occasion as if to say: You have told me your qualities of forgiveness, now You have a good opportunity to display them! (Num. 14.18). It reappears in Psalm 103 (vv. 8–10), with the threats at the end entirely removed and an even greater emphasis on God's willingness to forgive:

> Loving and gracious is the Eternal,
> long-suffering and full of faithful love.
> *Not* for all time does He accuse,
> *not* forever does He keep His anger,
> *not* according to our failings has He dealt with us,
> *not* according to our deceit has He treated us.

This slightly odd word order is to indicate the way the Hebrew begins each of the final four sentences with an emphatic negative, as if wiping out totally the remotest threat of punishment implied in the original passage. Indeed this tradition of amending this text to make it even more compassionate led the creators of the Jewish liturgy for festivals and particularly the Day of Atonement to omit part of the closing phrase 'not proclaiming the guilty innocent' so that it now reads simply 'proclaiming innocent' or 'making everyone fully innocent again'. The passage was clearly a most powerful statement of God's boundless love, a love through which the very survival of Israel was ultimately guaranteed. But what happens to it in the Book of Jonah?

Precisely at the point where his anger at the saving of Nineveh is being discussed, Jonah hurls these loving qualities back into God's face as if they were a sort of curse:

> Isn't this just what I said when I was back home! That's why I took off and fled to Tarshish, for I knew you were a God, gracious and loving, long-suffering and full of faithful love and forgiving of evil!

Think of the petulant, ungenerous character of Jonah by all means, but think also of the courage of the author to put this blasphemous affront to God's qualities into the mouth of his creation – and think of the courage of the compilers who kept it in the canon. Risking is everything in matters of faith.

All of which is a sort of preliminary to another sort of risk entirely. It is one thing to write a descriptive book on how the Bible might be analysed, and indeed to recommend a more creative approach to the text, including welcoming attempts to interpret it into other artistic modes, but it is something else to try to do so yourself. But if I cannot myself 'risk' being a little creative in working with the Bible, then this whole enterprise is a little dishonest.

The following passages flow directly from the Bendorf Jewish-Christian Bible Week. One of the few privileges I have kept for myself is the opportunity to preach there the Shabbat morning sermon. It is always difficult to find time to prepare it in the middle of all the other activities there, but it has become for me a kind of touchstone over the years. Am I still sensitive to what is going on in the Week so that the sermon really meets the experiences and needs of those participating? Is it still alive for me as well? While most of them have been fairly conventional exercises, I have sometimes used the opportunity to try a more imaginative or dramatic way of responding to the texts we have been studying. The following are a couple of examples.

When we studied the life of Solomon, I found myself increasingly frustrated trying to discover the man behind the vast number of 'monuments' with which he is surrounded both in life and in the text. He is also such a mixture of contradictions – being supposedly very wise yet at the same time managing to end up with the reputation in the Bible as a profligate and idolater. Incidentally, this so worried the Rabbis that the midrash has him being replaced on the throne temporarily by a demon (responsible for all his wrongdoings) while Solomon had to wander around the world in temporary exile. Hence the following 'autobiographical' statement.

I Solomon

I Solomon, by the grace of God, king of Israel, to hereby state in my defence . . . Or do I? Is it not too late to worry about what the old lawgiver once said about kings? What's done is done. I stand condemned if that is how you wish to see it. For does it not say in the fifth book of Moses, our Lawgiver beginning 'These are the words' that kings must tread warily on this precarious throne of Israel? 'Only let him not multiply horses . . . only let him not multiply wives . . . and as for silver and gold, let him not multiply these too much.' Forget about kings and these are familiar friends: power, sex and money, our constant companions through life.

Whoever has never wielded power let him be wary of making sermons about it. I know that old seducer power. I tasted it, and fought for it and held it – and I gave it up and let go, when the time was right. I know its promises and its reality. Without it we were nothing. Less than nothing. David left a half-finished world that was about to fall back into chaos. Revolts from our 'allies', jealousies within – if the old man had lingered on another year, he'd have seen the whole thing lost. They don't understand. Power is the purest priesthood there is. To suppress each private wish, subsume each desire to that great endless need. When to act and when to hold back. How to recognize and admit mistakes. How to hold on when you know you are right. When to be ruthless and when to make space for others. And whom do you trust? On whom do you rely? And how do you sleep, and how do you watch each change, each nuance, each hint of trouble? Paranoid? Of course I was paranoid – but at least I knew it, and learned to face reality. To hold the balance. For forty years to keep it going. And peace! Oh what a tired word! Yes, peace of a sort – they got so used to it they never saw how close we were to destruction at any moment. And they complained! The taxes are too high – too many conscripts – I was ruining the labour market! What did they think? It would cost nothing? Oh yes, alliances with Egypt, alliances with Tyre, marriages with all and sundry. Who needs an army, more chariots, more fortresses? Did they not know how close we were to the edge? A new Pharaoh; some barbarian tribe from the north; even our wretched 'allies' could gang up in a hurry – and goodbye Shlomo and Jerusalem and Temple. The creatures I took to my bed! for the good of those priests who complained about some pathetic stone idols. God save me from my clergy.

Did I abuse it? Is it time for honesty? Even if it were not I'd have to say 'yes'. Oh, sometimes I knew it and took a calculated risk. I don't count Joab and Adonijah – even that sneaky worm Shimei. Survival is survival. But sending those workers into Tyre against Hiram's wishes – that was a chance. I bet that scared him for a few moments. Was David back on the scene, gobbling up kingdoms like a locust? No, those were part of the game. But the abuses *I* know about, I kept off the record. Heavens, I needed a little self-indulgence once in a while. And *that* was dangerous. A little man can commit little sins – but a king . . . worlds can topple and kingdoms split apart.

They wanted a king and I gave them a king. Power, glory, pride. I inherited a peasant confederacy – no trust, no loyalty, no unity. And I left them a state, a force in the world. I gave them culture from Egypt, technology from the Philistines, commerce from Tyre, religion from . . . well let us say 'God' and not be too particular. No, more than that! Much more! Power, sex and money. I gave them the antidotes, the secrets of living in a halfway civilized manner. I gave them wisdom – proverbs practical and theoretical, public and private. And then taught them how to bring wisdom under the banner of their God: 'It is a tree of life to those who grasp it.' Wisdom is become Torah – and there is no question that cannot be asked, no truth that cannot be accepted, no risk the mind dare not take. That I gave them for 'power'.

And I gave them a book of love songs – the only time I really beat the old man at his own game. It will have its uses. They'll need to break their own taboos and fears and superstitions. I saved the heart – not to mention the loins – for God, may he be praised.

And then the old master of assemblies. 'Vanity of vanities.' That's the one they never understood. I gave them the blessing of scepticism. At least, I made it religiously respectable. Sceptical about everything – our big truths and little ones, our values, our 'assured results of scholarship', our economic systems. Of course it hurts – but I saved those single-minded enthusiasts from ever becoming fanatics, and for that they should bless my grave every day.

I had one sin. I freely admit it. And that is the other reason I left no personal account for history. I hid instead behind my buildings, my wealth, my army, my speeches and my Temple, because I could not show my real face. The sin? You'll be disappointed I assure you. You see: I had no sense of humour. Oh there was irony – more than enough for the whole dynasty. But David robbed me of humour. Surviving the old man's curses, his irrationality, his favourites, his promises. That robbed me of the power to laugh. And he was the poet – that I envy him. I wrote prose – prose writ large and monumental. Temples, fortresses, palaces, stables. I taught them pride. I gave them security. I wrote their history. I created their culture. I wrote in stone across the face of the land and I spread their story across the length and breadth of the world. But in prose, prose, always prose. Oh David, David, you hateful father. Why did

you die so soon and never see it? I built it for you, all for you. Your
Temple for your God. I, the youngest, the last, the child of your sin.
Who had to prove so much – damn it, I did it. I took your rabble of
herdsmen and peasants and farmers and traders and I dragged them
into the light of a new world. I gave them a culture, a society, a
history. I gave them wit and colour, and enormous curiosity. I gave
them choice – and that was the only, but the greatest, mistake. They
learned to think – enough to smash it all. 'There was a little city with
few inhabitants and a great king came and surrounded it, and built
great siegeworks against it. But there was found within it a man,
poor but wise, who delivered the city through his wisdom. But no
one remembered that poor, unfortunate man . . . Wisdom is
greater than weapons of war – but one fool can destroy a lot of
good.' (Eccles. 9.14f., 18).

One fool can do a lot of harm. In the end you may not accept these
my words – but they are simple and true. There are only these three
old friends that stand in the way: power, sex and money. That is why
the old lawgiver knew he had to transmute them: 'Love the Eternal
your God with all your heart, and with all your soul and with all your
might.' All having been said, this is not even piety – it is common
sense and survival.

But do not speak of this love too often, and make no claim to
understand it. For you will come to trust yourself too much, and
your 'heart', 'soul' and 'might' could turn into their other selves,
'power', 'sex' and 'money', and destroy you.

I have left behind no horses, no wives, no silver and gold. But the
memory of them will live forever – to trouble you, oh, how they will
trouble you!

The testament of Solomon, king in Jerusalem, is ended.

For two years we worked in Bendorf with the first twelve chapters of
Isaiah, and I found myself composing the following curious piece,
something after the manner of a *Times* obituary. To appreciate it
you may care to study these chapters. Despite the slightly peculiar
conclusions I seem to have come to, they can all be justified, more
or less, by the text itself.

Isaiah Ben Amotz

I can imagine a different Isaiah. He was born into the upper classes,
child of a priestly family. Of considerable intelligence he was
spotted early on as a potential leader within his society. In addition

to the regular education reserved for the priesthood – which included reading, writing, elementary scribal arts, basic biology and medicine – he attended the schools set aside for those destined for the government administration, with the possibility one day of entering the diplomatic service. However, at an early stage, a perceptive teacher noted a tendency in the young man to be not merely creative as a writer, but to have moments of extra-sensory experience and trance-like states. This led to a radical redirection in his life into one of the several prophetic training schools in Jerusalem. Here, in addition to his grounding in covenant traditions, legal and cultic matters, he studied the wisdom teachings and also the secrets of the prophetic mysteries – including meditation techniques, special ritual and prayer rites, fasting and self-induced ecstatic or out-of-body states.

Despite his considerable gifts and early promise, over the years such psychic abilities as he had as a child disappeared – perhaps due to his phenomenal intellectual development and his increasing interest in literature and poetry. From an early age he had composed remarkable passages for the Temple, describing the qualities of God with a refined theological expression and insight that both shocked and drew the admiration of the Levitical schools and, more importantly, the upper echelons of the Priesthood. It was that support, and his own family connections behind the scenes (which he did not know about until some years later) that led to the adoption of his famous '*kadosh kadosh kadosh*' (holy, holy, holy) into the liturgy for festive occasions. The threefold repetition of the '*kadosh*' was considered a remarkably daring innovation, and at the time a wit among the Levites suggested that once they had got over the shock, the very angels would sing the passage in the heavenly court. It must be said that when Isaiah heard the joke he found it hard to suppress a blush of pleasure. The composition had come to him so much like a divine revelation that he was willing to accept heavenly endorsement as a possibility. In later years he came to regret this conceit.

But in his late twenties he found himself more and more drawn into court politics and drifting further and further from the classroom of the prophetic schools where he had already acquired some teaching experience in homiletics, communication skills and elementary rhetoric. It was in the court, in the circles of the royal policy-making bodies, that he found his intelligence most stretched. He enjoyed discussing military tactics with the general staff (of whom he did not think a great deal as strategists but whose tales of prowess he secretly admired). He enjoyed the diplomatic niceties of the current negotiations with the Northern Kingdom, while keeping a line open to the newly emergent Assyrian Empire. In these circles the young man found that the respect shown to his opinions and the admiration given to the poems and occasional dramatized readings that he prepared, gave him enormous satisfaction and not a little pride.

Though he was reluctant to admit it, the favours granted to him by the young women who adorned the court were also flattering, and far removed from the somewhat ascetic elements of his former prophetic training and the self-discipline usually encouraged among the younger members of the priestly families. At all events his career in either the upper ranks of the diplomatic corps, the civil service or the royal household seemed assured.

And then came the fateful experience that literally changed his life overnight. The death of King Uzziah was not unexpected following his long illness. Though sad and, like many of his contemporaries, a little uneasy about the political future under the new regime, Isaiah also recognized the opportunities for advancement in the new situation. He was particularly pleased when he learned that they would be chanting the '*kadosh*' in a new setting during the enthronement ceremony. If anything was likely to get the young religious poet and courtier noticed it was this prominent exposure.

Nothing in the earlier part of the ritual prepared him for what was to follow. As the smoke of the incense rose in the inner chamber of the sanctuary, there fell upon him a dizziness and trembling that he had not known since his earliest childhood experiences. Not any of the techniques of his various prophetic and priestly disciplines had prepared him for the overwhelming sensation that overcame him. It was as if the very walls of the Temple shook and dissolved about him. The smoke of the incence thickened, became almost tangible, filling the room, or rather the entire open space now about him and almost suffocating him with its closeness. The temporary throne brought in for such state occasions seemed to rise before his eyes and splinter into a myriad sparkling lights. (In later years he was loathe to go into too much detail about what he saw because he was embarrassed at the vulgarity of the vision.) But what drew his attention and held it with dreadful power were the moving fiery figures that now fluttered about the heavenly throne where formerly his familiar priestly colleagues had stood. And upon the throne, both visible and invisible, drawing his eyes and blinding him at the same time, was manifest the presence of the Eternal God of Hosts, the Holy One of Israel, the Mighty One of Jacob.

At that moment the security, smugness and naive wisdom of the young man fell away, and he found himself utterly naked and pathetic, worse yet, vile, grotesque and absurd, in that Presence. The wit, the rhetoric and social graces were burned out of him and his overwhelming sensation was one of shame, of wasted years and talents, of the utter folly and futility of all he had achieved. And in a moment of dreadful clarity, helped by his native irony, he understood as never before the real implications of the great 'kadosh' he had so lightly called his own. For God was indeed utterly beyond anything he could even begin to conceive of, and even the majestic ritual of the Temple and the ages of tradition that lay behind it were mere absurd gestures of piety before the One. Yet he also knew with certainty that there was indeed no part of the life of this world, of his people, of his own insignificant person, that was not filled, given value and meaning, by the weight of God's presence.

The account he left (Isa. 6) is too well known to need repeating. He was later to be criticized for his assertion that his people too were of unclean lips. He had seen it as an excuse. How could he be better than he was, given the people out of whom he came? His contemporaries, particularly in the priesthood, were too mindful of their task of keeping the people in a state of sufficient purity for ritual purposes, to accept his explanation with much enthusiasm. It may even be that that mistake cost him the ear of those who might have accepted some of his legitimate criticisms of the Temple cult, particularly the rather excessive attention paid to those with money and power, however dubious the sources of their wealth.

But there is nothing more disturbing to authority than a critique from within. This promising young man, who seemed groomed to fill an important role within the establishment, became utterly impossible in the wake of this mysterious experience. What had been accepted as a mild talent to amuse became quite unacceptable when he satirized every aspect of the hierarchy: priestly, legal, military, political, prophetic and royal. His insistence on taking literally the covenant promises, and indeed its sanctions, and his newly-found isolationist political views, were received with irritation and ultimately anger.

What his opponents could not see was that Isaiah himself was no less horrified than they were by his newly found voice. The last thing in the world he wanted was to find himself at odds with all the institutions and values that he had spent his lifetime serving and asserting. It is true that his training gave him the precise equipment needed to question and criticize the very heart of his society. His perception of corruption was based on a thoroughgoing experience of every group he attacked. In fact what he had noted in a mildly humorous way before, now burst out of him with a corruscating fury that terrified him no less than it enthralled him. In the first phase of his newly-discovered understanding he was utterly one-sided, devastating and ferocious in his attack on the things he had for so long loved, supported and underpinned. He was probably only saved by his refined aesthetic sense that ultimately refused to allow him to produce second-rate polemic where first-rate poetic invective was needed. The creator of '*kadosh*' could turn his hand to a dramatized chorus of warning that human pride would fall and God's power rise (Isa. 2.5–22); to a sound poem, ironically celebrating the meaningless ornamentation of the ladies of the court (3.18–23); to a drunken rhythmic mimicry of the priests and prophets in their cups (28.7–8) and to a popular song about God's love for his vineyard (5.1–7) that assured him a place in the hearts of the people. Indeed this poetic gift, or even vocation, saved him from far more drastic treatment. Despite his criticisms he was eventually valued as someone to turn to for the divine word, even though it rarely accorded with the policy decisions of the ruling elite.

Throughout all the years of his second life as a political gadfly and public conscience, he lived under a double sense of challenge. Part of him saw an inevitable destruction coming to the society he knew. The symptoms already manifest in the Northern Kingdom, that were to lead to its destruction in his own days, were present before his eyes in the South, even though he was spared the time of collapse. But another part of him could see as clearly some other possibility for the future. A hope of some purified remnant surviving to fulfil God's will in a new, refined Israelite society. But he was to be haunted till his death by the fear that his would be the last voice to bring the necessary hope and warning to change his people's fate. He rarely displayed his private fears, but a hint can be found in the record he left of that revelation, when he called out to God in despair, 'How long?'

So he remained till the end a driven figure, forced against his better judgment, his temperament and training to stand outside the establishment he was born and bred to lead. He might have had an important career in government circles, or lived out his life as a noted poet and dramatist, with some significant liturgical compositions to his credit. Whether they would have survived is hard to tell. Strangely enough, the more powerful his prophetic writing the less he noticed its aesthetic worth and maybe it gained from that detachment.

In editing the first part of his collected writings he hesitated for a long time about what to call them. His training would have suggested the usual term '*divrey*', with its double sense of 'words' or 'matters'. But perhaps a little poetic conceit still remained, or perhaps he felt that the experience in the Temple had really transformed his talent from mere poetic trivia to some sort of universal truth. In the end he settled for '*hazon*', 'vision', for he truly saw what others could not or would not see. It seems to be the right term for a poet who, despite himself, became a prophet.

On one other occasion I tried to get 'into the skin' of the Bible itself and write something about the power it holds over me. In fact it was the specific trigger for writing this book. Hence the next chapter on 'revelation' and another kind of risking.

8

Revelation in the Hebrew Bible

Until now I have expressed myself with a relative degree of caution about the nature of the Bible itself. I find myself on this issue both open-minded and committed. 'My 'secular' side leaves me free to treat it as any other document – that is to say to bring to it any sort of evaluative technique that seems relevant and not feel that there are limitations that must be placed on this exploration. My 'religious' side, and I readily acknowledge this 'schizophrenia', reacts to it with a sense of awe and commitment that demands that I take it deeply seriously – though not necessarily in accord with classical Jewish tradition.

This dual nature of my approach is perhaps inevitable in what we call a secular age. I recall a story told me by Lionel Blue about three different lecturers he had when he did Jewish studies at University College in London. All three of them were in some measure traditional Jews, who nevertheless found themselves teaching scientific approaches to the sacred texts of the Bible. How did they cope? They each had two pockets, he thought. In one of them they kept their scholarship, in the other their tradition. One of them would take out his tradition and his scholarship, put them side by side look at them – and weep. The other would do the same thing, look at them – and laugh. Lionel never spoke about the solution of the third. Knowing him I suspect that he was the most integrated of the three, and much like Rav Sperber, enjoyed or suffered the intellectual struggle, without feeling religiously threatened. Of the other two, the one who 'laughed', later took his life.

Perhaps all modern religious people are caught between these polarities and we each come to terms in our own way, finding some position along the continuum. My greatest discomfort is with those who have newly discovered the religious and feel they have to deny even the existence, let alone the legitimacy, of any of the secular values that have shaped their lives until then. I have the same discomfort with 'born again' atheists. To deny the reality of things that have formed us is to remain their slave.

At a Jewish-Christian-Muslim conference, another dialogue situation that takes place annually in Bendorf, a young Muslim from a very strictly 'orthodox' background expressed his puzzlement about the conference at the closing session. 'I came here,' he said, 'expecting to find religious people, but instead I found secular people looking for religion.' Perhaps he saw this as a regrettable failure on our part, I found it both precise and comforting.

All of which is by way of introducing this chapter on revelation, which tries to express something of my own religious consciousness of the importance of the Hebrew Bible. The bulk of the chapter was originally presented to an Anglican-Jewish dialogue group which meets at the Sternberg Centre where my College is located. It was subsequently published in *Manna*, the magazine of the Centre, that is edited by Rabbi Tony Bayfield who is also one of the convenors of the group. It was the challenge of the group that encouraged me to formulate my views on this subject, and ultimately encouraged me to attempt this book. It is to Tony that I owe a question that suddenly pops up about a quarter of the way through.

At the time the paper evoked two responses that I am still trying to come to terms with. A Christian colleague found a piece which matched it to a quite remarkable extent, except for the New Testament overtones – written by a young Karl Barth. An Orthodox Rabbi, an old friend who is also part of the group, thought that it revealed me as a 'romantic fundamentalist'! I offer it here, unabridged apart from a couple of paragraphs that appear elsewhere in the book.

The Hebrew Bible is rarely self-conscious. It does not explain why it came into being, its purpose or its significance. It is not portentous as in the way of other ancient literatures that proclaim themselves as the authentic, official revelation of a particular god to, or through, his earthly regent. The Hebrew Bible takes for granted its own worth by assuming the worth of the one who reads it. It exposes itself with its naiveté and cunning, to a relationship, with the openness and concealment of a lover to the beloved. 'I am my beloved's and my beloved is mine' (Song of Songs 6.3).

In another context Arthur Miller has expressed the same view in terms of the artistic urge:

A play, even the angry and critical kind, is always on the one hand a love letter to the world, to which a loving acknowledgment is eagerly awaited.[1]

Thus to talk of 'revelation' in the Hebrew Bible is on a certain level absurd. As the mystics have argued, the Bible itself is the revelation of God. Every letter, let alone words and sentences, is somehow an act of divine self-exposure, of intimacy and vulnerability. The technicalities of genre: narrative, poetry, prophecy, law, wisdom, history, name-lists, building instructions, are merely faces that reflect and thus address the broadest human experience. That is why the Hebrew Bible accepts no conflict between 'revelation' and 'reason' (Ecclesiastes), nor rejects the worlds of emotion and sensuality (Song of Songs). They all blend together as one. They become in their totality, to borrow Hermann Cohen's phrase about religious ritual, 'gestures of love'.

Thus the 'God' of many names and identities who appears within the pages is not 'revealed' in some ultimate sense at certain specified moments and places. There are indeed many such moments and places within the narratives, though different traditions have put weight on some more than on others. The God of the Hebrew Bible can appear in a story, or speak through a prophet, or be seen indirectly through a vision, or be addressed passionately by an anonymous poet. But this 'God' is still only a character like all the others, all of whom together are only aspects and faces of the same truth. The crude text we have before us can only hint at realities and possibilities to be met and experienced in the exploration of a relationship that transcends it.

Since the 'crude text' is our starting point, however it came down to us in its present form, we must make of it what we can. In fact, so dangerous is it that no tradition has actually dared let it alone but has clothed it, or smothered it, in finery. The very choice of the sequence of individual books within the Bible reflects the process both of understanding and of control.

Within Jewish tradition the three layers of text that make up the *tenakh* are accorded varying degrees of sanctity. The core, the Torah, is seen as directly revealed through Moses without his

---

[1]Arthur Miller, *Timebends: A Life*, Methuen 1987, p. 243.

personality impacting upon it. However, the *neviim*, the prophetic books, Joshua to Malachi, are 'composed' by specific authors and therefore 'mediated' by them. The rabbinic view that 'No two prophets prophesied in the same style' (Babylonian Talmud, Sanhedrin 89a), as we have noted before, suggests that the individual perceptions, experiences, human qualities and failings, even literary style, of the prophet affect what he sees or hears and records of God's word. Thus these books form an outer ring to Torah, one stage removed from the centre. The *ketuvim*, the 'writings', Psalms to Chronicles, which form the outermost ring, are 'inspired' by the *ruah hakodesh*, the 'holy spirit' – the balance of divine-human relationship shifts further towards the human end. If Torah and *neviim* are God's words to human beings, then *ketuvim* are human responses or appeals, human self-revelation, to God.

'But is not the Bible also, at times, boring, repetitive, offensive, narrow, disturbing, blind and, the greatest of all contemporary sins, unhistorical?'

It may well be but it is the nature of such books of revelation and to some extent a proof that they are indeed 'revelation', that they challenge in different ways successive generations of readers, both because of and despite the discomfort they arouse. They remain alive to the critical, aesthetic, scientific, philosophical or other enquiries that are laid before them with gentle piety or hurled at them with all the violence and passion we can muster. There are passages, whole books, that may be dead for centuries, or treated to the distancing of allegory so as to allow them to retain any power or authority. Others may offend a contemporary morality – and not only that of the late twentieth century. Every generation has similarly been forced to find strategies for defending or disarming or flatly contradicting the sacred word. But the imperative to exercise such options is a further reminder of the troubling potency of the source. And sometimes a text can explode into symbolic power in a way utterly new and unexpected. Who can read the tale of Abimelech in Judges 9 today without trembling at its prophetic perception of the rise of a Hitler? How has the image of Noah's ark become suddenly alive and poignant since we awoke to the ecological crises facing our fragile 'spaceship earth'?

Perhaps as impressive as the work of the composers or compilers of the original volumes of our Bible is the revelatory intuition and courage of those who selected and preserved the canon. And surely it is still a confirmation of the potency of a text that its apparent unhistoricity or amorality can produce in us frustration or anger. For it points to and evokes a human quest for truth, integrity and purity. The scandal of a biblical passage's apparent failure to live up to the highest current qualities and values of a particular generation may become the trigger for their own self-transcendence. Such struggles to vindicate the text are all the more heroic in their intensity and consequences because they have to contradict what was previously regarded as the highest of human and religious values as enshrined in previous interpretations. The Bible continually subverts itself and sanctions self-criticism through its own overt content. 'Take away from me your songs . . . rather let justice roll down like water' (Amos 5.23–24).

Surprisingly the Bible has survived the onslaught of even the most critical scholarship of the last centuries. It is not challenge that harms it but uncritical piety or indifference. True, the authenticity or legitimacy of the whole could be challenged by whittling away at enough of the parts. A contemporary Canon Revision Working Party would have jettisoned: Song of Songs – too erotic; Joshua, Judges and much of Samuel and Kings – too violent; Leviticus – irrelevant cult; Ecclesiastes – too cynical; many prophetic passages – too obscure; much of Exodus, Numbers and Deuteronomy – too legalistic or repetitive; Esther – too particularistic; Lamentations – too depressing; Job – too blasphemous; many Proverbs – too materialistic. We might salvage Ruth, Psalm 23 and a few stories in Genesis, suitably censored. If the text as we have it is the given, then in its totality, as a record of the human struggle to understand the word of God, it stands exposed before us, inviting a meeting.

God remains concealed. The text itself urges caution in seeking to encounter God directly. 'None may see my face and live', or, perhaps more accurately, 'no living person may see my face' (Ex. 33.20). But more radically, the text itself contains a variety of literary devices that effectively preserve the distance between human perception and divine reality.

There is a narrative technique common to the stories of Abraham's meeting with the three men/angels (Gen. 18), to Moses at the burning bush (Ex. 3) and even to Sinai itself (Ex. 19; 24). It allows the reader to know simultaneously the facts of there being a divine manifestation and, at the same time, the limited subjective experiences of the character or people who actually witness it. We, the readers, recognize the distance between what they 'see' and what is really going on. Moses 'sees' a bush burning but not consumed; the reader knows there is an 'angel of the Eternal' present within it, though we are none the wiser about what an 'angel/messenger' (Hebrew: *malakh*) really means. There is 'revelation' to an individual but what is 'revealed' is so far less than the truth that even from our privileged perspective we can only be impressed and disturbed at the same time. The mysterious, *ehyeh asher ehyeh*, 'I am that I am' that God says to Moses at the bush (Ex. 3.14) may lead to many philosophical and mystical interpretations, but, in its grammatical essence, it means: 'I am only known to myself', or, more bluntly, 'Mind your own business!' We learn at the same moment both the possibility and impossibility of revelation.

According to George Steiner, Schoenberg in his opera *Moses and Aaron* expressed the same paradox. In the opera, Moses only speaks, while Aaron, his spokesperson, sings. The prophet who has the closest experience of God is the man of 'heavy tongue' who knows he cannot express the truth of what he has experienced of God. But Aaron can select from that experience enough to give it popular expression. Moses keeps the truth but cannot speak; Aaron can speak but the very act of speaking betrays the truth. Moses points to God; Aaron leads to the Golden Calf.

Jewish tradition is no less cautious on this matter, though different strands will react in different ways. The legitimacy of the covenant with God is affirmed in Midrash by the fact that 600,000 adult males witnessed the giving of the Torah at Sinai. But the Hebrew terms for the event are singularly cautious. There is no traditional Hebrew expression for the English phrase 'revelation at Mount Sinai'. Instead we have the phrase *ma'amad har sinai*, the 'standing at Mount Sinai'. At least we can anchor the human component of the event in some sort of reality – we stood there. Similarly the festival of *shavuot*, Pentecost, that celebrates the event, is designated as *zeman matan toratenu*, 'the time of the giving of our Torah'. After all, we define ourself as a people through our possession of, and indeed the content of, the Torah. But we adhere very strongly to the assertion in Deuteronomy, 'you heard the sound of words, but saw no form' (Deut. 4.12). We acknowledge the tangible gift which takes for granted a giver.

Like the passages mentioned above, texts after Genesis go to great lengths to put an angel or other messenger between the hero and God. In the stories of Gideon in Judges 6 or the parents of Samson in Judges 13, there is even a sort of folk humour in the telling. They 'know' on some level they have met an angel, but it requires a miraculous disappearance before they can actually believe it. We laugh at their discomfort; God is playful with such simple people. But a further lesson is also driven home: the moment we become self-conscious or possessive about the encounter with the Divine it vanishes and we must act in trust that what we experienced was true. It happened, if we allow it to have consequences. Like prophecy itself, it can only be verified retroactively.

Most dramatic, considering his ability to conjure up miracles, is the celebrated experience of Elijah. The violent God he calls on to withhold the rain, or to bring down fire from heaven to devour the sacrifice, is ultimately revealed in a single, simple question and in silence, after all the natural and supernatural phenomena have passed. 'But the Eternal was not in the wind . . . or the earthquake . . . or the fire' (I Kings 19.11–22). Elijah can make no new response to that silence and merely repeats in identical words his previous self-justification (compare I Kings 19.10 with 19.14). So he is passed over and must appoint his successor Elisha (I Kings 19.16). An insistent voice that awaits an answer is the biblical expression of God's presence, not revealed to the eye but heard by the inner ear (compare Jonah 1.1–2 and 3.1–2). Elijah's 'sound of thinly-sliced silence' – not really a 'still small voice' – is a final comment on the meaning of all the miracles in the Hebrew Bible. Some may be necessary to get the 'children' out of trouble, crossing the Reed Sea, thirsting in the desert, but they, too, are ultimately dangerous. The manifestation, the revelation, must not be confused with God. The universe cannot be expected to change its laws for human convenience. That way too leads to idolatry.

The Rabbis taught that the dividing of the Reed Sea and the standing still of the sun for Joshua were pre-ordained and built into the universe in advance by God (Genesis Rabbah 5.5). Alongside these, as we have already noted, were Jonah's miraculous fish and Balaam's talking donkey – created in the twilight between the end of the sixth day of Creation and the Shabbat. Hillel taught that the process whereby we get our daily bread is a greater miracle than the crossing of the Reed Sea (Pesikta Rabbati 152a).

Either everything is revelation or nothing.

A verse in the Book of Numbers (7.89) has been interpreted along these lines. 'When Moses used to enter the tent of meeting to speak with God, he heard the voice, *meeddabber*, speaking to him.' This form of the verb 'to speak' is unusual. One might expect a *piel* (the 'intensive' form of the Hebrew verb usually used for the verb *dibber*, to speak) participle – 'speaking', but the grammatical form suggests instead a *hitpael* or 'reflexive' form of the verb. That would mean that God was 'speaking to himself'. Moses entered to find God talking to himself all the time. The word of God is always present, waiting to be heard. It is just that no one is listening.

The point can be taken even further. There is no guarantee that the word will be heard correctly even by the most 'qualified' of listeners. The Hebrew Bible abounds with tales of true and false prophets in conflict over the meaning of God's word. The ones we accept as 'true' represent a minority. Their audience would have been utterly bewildered by the conflicting views of seemingly authentic spokespersons of God and usually chosen against the ones the Bible ultimately recognized as being right. (We will see an example of this in the struggle between Jeremiah and Hananiah.)

We can also see the problem in a simple narrative example. The prophet Samuel stands at a major transitional point in the biblical narrative, for he marks the change from leadership by judges to the establishment of a monarchy. But Samuel's personal judgment becomes crucial in his later relationship with the tragic figure of Saul, for it is hard to know how far his rejection of the people's wish for a king colours his treatment of the tall, young man he selects. But that is to psychologize. The text is more blunt. When choosing a son of Jesse as Saul's successor, Samuel again goes for the tall, firstborn son (I Sam. 16.13), to be reminded sharply by God that God sees to the heart, not the outer appearance. The prophet can get it wrong! That scandalous truth is enormously threatening to us who have inherited the Hebrew Bible. If a prophet can be wrong, then anything can be wrong and no word is guaranteed. Or rather, responsibility is thrown back upon us at the point where we had assumed the risk was removed.

Again, Arthur Miller in *Timebends*:

> Before the idol, men remain dependent children. Before God they are burdened and at the same time liberated to participate in the decisions of endless creation (p. 259).

If prophets can make mistakes, the decision remains with us. Revelation is too important and too dangerous to be left to the experts.

If the Hebrew Bible is a love letter, it contains such passion as would devour the most ardent lover. The recurrent image of God as the betrayed lover jostles with that of the loving parent bound to forgive its errant child. We feel a constant tug of emotions, of love given, expected, unrequited, denied or betrayed, love at once tender or devoted and ferocious and devouring. It is not the revelation of God that is to be looked for – it is there throughout in all its nakedness and hopelessness. But where is the revelation of human beings in response, where is that love returned?

It is there, but in individual voices. The seeming confidence of Abraham is astonishingly powerful. Love and trust enough to set aside all human ties and the assumptions of human love. A silent Isaac can offer his life. A Jacob can struggle in the dark with his own nightmares and guilts and failures – and find in this his own way to God. Amos can abandon his herds and Elisha his family land. Countless prophets can give their lives; Hannah can surrender her long-desired child. Jeremiah can call God to account. Job can face the whirlwind. David can submit his drive and ambition and lust before a God who demands his sons, one by one. The unknown Psalmists can cry out their longing 'in a dry and weary land where there is no water' or, in ultimate trust, take shelter under God's all-embracing wings. And once the people too, as a whole, can make the intuitive leap of acceptance into a commitment that they must spend millennia seeking to understand. 'We will do what we have heard' they say at Sinai (Ex. 24.7). The divine self-love is mediated and somehow fulfilled through its own creation. Creator and creatures celebrate their union before settling into the rigours and realities of marriage, the growing apart and together, the loving and hating, the learning to listen, to yield, to yell, to feel the loneliness of rejection and separation and the ecstasy of return and reunion. 'When love was strong' said the Rabbis, 'we could have made our bed on a sword's blade; now, when it has become weak, a bed of sixty cubits is not large enough for us.'

The Zohar, the central work of Jewish mysticism, captures the mystery of this relationship:

> It is like a girl, beautiful and gracious and much loved and she is kept closely confined in her palace. She has a special lover, unrecognized by anyone and concealed. This lover, because of the love which he feels for her, passes by the door of her house, and looks on every side and she knows that her lover is constantly walking to and fro by the door of her house. What does she do? She opens a tiny door in the secret palace where she lives and shows her face to her lover. Then she withdraws at once and is

gone. None of those in her lover's vicinity sees or understands but her lover alone knows and his heart and soul and inner being yearn for her and he knows that it is because of the love that she bears him that she showed herself to him for a moment, in order to awaken love in him.

So it is with the Torah. She reveals herself only to her lover. The Torah knows that the wise man walks to and fro every day by the door of her house. What does she do? She shows her face to him from the palace and signals to him and she withdraws at once to her palace, and hides herself. None of those who are there knows or understands but he alone knows and his heart and soul and inner being yearn for her. And so the Torah is revealed and then is hidden and treats her lover lovingly, in order to awaken love in him. (The Zohar, Mishpatim 99a, trans. David Goldstein)

Those bound together know absence and reconciliation and a million moods in between, moments that reveal the self and the other, presence and absence – a continuum of shared experience. 'My beloved is mine and I am his' (Song of Songs 2.16). Only the onlooker, the outsider, asks about 'revelation'. For God and Israel, for those in love, no place exists without it. 'For love is strong as death; its flames are flames of fire, a very flame of the Eternal' (Song of Songs 8.6).

PART TWO

The Old Questions, The Old Answers

9

Leaving the Garden – Did They Fall or Were They Pushed?

We do not know from the Bible why God chose to create human beings and the world. The first two chapters of Genesis may be separate compositions or complementary parts of the same drama – but they give us no clear idea. Human beings are defined as sharing with God something of the divine, an image, a breath – but they are also earth, an idea reinforced by the word-play on Adam and *adamah* (ground) – a play, incidentally, that also includes an allusion to redness (*edom*) and blood (*dam*). We have a dual nature – earth and spirit; we share with our Creator the ability to form and mould (*yatzar* in the Hebrew), though the term *bara* (to create – as 'In the beginning God *created*') is restricted in Hebrew to God alone. We are formed to 'serve', or 'work' the earth (another word play) and to guard it. One of the Jewish commentators of this century, Benno Jacob, suggests that since this was the purpose of the creation of human beings, the entire Eden episode was only a test to show us that no other kind of life was possible for us. We failed the test and had to leave paradise to take up our proper place and work in the world. Perhaps it is this reason that accounts for the tone of the Fall story. It is not one of anger or righteous indignation on the part of God – though some traditions seem to see it that way. It has, instead, a sense of irony, a deeply felt awareness of an impossible dream that could never be sustained.

Let us look a bit more closely at the key moments of downfall, the dialogue between the serpent and Eve.

The Eternal God has created a garden in Eden, filled it with plants and trees, and placed Adam within it. He gives him one command:

Of every tree of the garden you may surely eat.
But of the tree of the knowledge of good and evil you shall not eat

of it – for on the day you eat of it, you will surely die (Gen. 2.16–
17)

Why this restriction on Adam's freedom? In part it is a test, and
yet in part it is intended presumably for Adam's own good. After
all, the very next verse tells of God's concern that the man should
not be alone and the search God undertakes to find him a suitable
partner. Nor is the death that God mentions necessarily a threat or
punishment – as it stands before us in the Hebrew text it is merely a
statement of fact. It clearly does not mean that on the very day they
eat they shall die, for first of all they do not do so, and anyway the
Hebrew idiom should not be taken literally. Something about
eating the fruit will change their awareness of the death that is
ultimately theirs – they will live with the knowledge of its
inevitability, of the finiteness of their life. But that knowledge is still
ahead of them.

What is the 'knowledge of good and evil'? A number of
possibilities present themselves to us if we look at the use of this
phrase in the Bible. According to Deut. 1.39, it is children who do
not know the difference between 'good and evil', so perhaps we are
talking about some stage in life before certain distinctions can be
made. Very often commentators have tried to see this as a moral
sense and, of course, a whole superstructure of interpretation of the
meaning as being primarily sexual still weighs heavily on many
people. But this is the unlikeliest of all interpretations. Elsewhere
we find David described as someone who is 'like the angel of God to
discern good and evil' (II Sam. 14.17). But, in the parallel passage
which comes later on, we read: 'But my lord has wisdom like the
angel of God to know *all things that are on earth*' (v. 20). That is to
say: the two words 'good' and 'evil' cover two extremes and
everything in between; it is 'knowledge' of all possibilities that we
are talking of here – that is, the potentiality that lies before Adam, if
he will eat of the fruit – and it is from this knowledge that God
wishes to preserve him.

The snake turns its attention to Eve. Again, what motivates it is
unclear. We only know of its cunning, a word (*arom*) which plays on
the word for nakedness (*arumim*) in the previous sentence (compare 3.1 and 2.25). Incidentally, it is important to note here a
distinction between the Hebrew Bible in its earliest Jewish version
and what Christians have done with it through chapter divisions. In
the Hebrew Bible, the story of the snake follows on from what has

gone before without a break – so that there is a unit from the beginning of chapter 2 (v. 4): 'These are the generations of the heaven and earth', up to the closing part of chapter 3 where God makes clothes for the man and his wife (3.21). It is only the Christian chapter divisions, presumably because of the later importance attached to the story of the Fall, that make the artificial division at the beginning of chapter 3, thus isolating the episode of the snake.

The snake asks its seemingly innocent question of the woman: 'Did God say that you cannot eat of all the trees of the Garden?' Is it seeking clarification of a puzzling matter? That is the tone it adopts, according to Benno Jacob. After all, no such prohibition exists for the animals, and it only wants to be sure. Perhaps the snake is only one of the de-mythologized primaeval serpents of other Near Eastern mythologies – those that fought with God for mastery of the world. Here it is relegated to a creature like others formed by God, and its rebellion reduced to a seduction. Yet its question already contains the seed of the failure to come.

Eve's answer seems accurate and sensible at first glance.

Of the fruit of the trees of the garden we may eat. Only of the fruit of the tree which is in the midst of the garden did God say: You shall not eat of it nor touch it lest you die (3.2–3).

The snake has given her the chance to correct it, to be right – though she goes too far in adding the prohibition on touching the tree. (Was that her idea or Adam's? God did not say it. The Rabbis thought that Adam had added it as a way of putting a 'fence around the Torah', that is to say, to create a secondary regulation that would prevent the risk of her even getting near to the fruit. So the Rabbis had the snake push her so that she fell against the tree and touched it – nothing happened! If that is the case, nothing will happen if you eat it as well! This is clearly a reflection on their own concern with the law-making process and the risk of making the 'fence' bigger than the law it is designed to protect. If laws become more honoured in the breach, people lose their respect for the law itself.)

Eve makes another slight change: the certainty of God's remark that on the day they eat of it they shall die becomes softened to 'in case you die'. But in essentials she is right. Yet something else has happened in this moment, as she begins to focus her attention on the mysterious tree. For she has defended God against the insinuation of the snake – and to defend someone means taking into oneself the criticism that one is refuting. The question has been raised about God's conduct and the snake's subsequent remarks only open wider the door that has already been unlocked. For Eve no longer stands within a closed world in which her obedience of God is unquestioned and assumed. She has defended God and so, for a brief moment, she has stepped outside the old situation – she has seen God's commandment from a new perspective and she can no longer return to her previous state. It is like the situation of a child. In its earliest years it obeys or does not, behaves or does not, as it tests out its emerging personality against the forces of parental authority that control it, learning something of its freedom and the limitations on that. But then there comes a time when other authorities appear, and the child begins to get a different view of parents whose power is no longer total, whose knowledge is no longer all-embracing, whose authority is no longer absolute. The child begins to grow up and take responsibility itself for its life.

Eve is on the threshold of such a moment. The snake's response is as much her own one on this journey towards independence. For, if God's command can be questioned, then so can His motivation, and Eve moves from simple, unquestioning obedience to judgment of God's conduct itself.

> God knows that on the day you eat of it your eyes will be opened and you will be like God, knowing good and evil.

The snake speaks enough truth to convince, for indeed their eyes will be opened – though in what sense they will become like God as a result is not too clear. So, after much reflection on the different qualities of the fruit, the woman eats and gives to her husband.

What I am trying to suggest is that in a way the 'Fall' was completed before they ate the fruit. The act itself was only a seal on a process that had already begun with the snake's first question and Eve's defence of God. Perhaps it really goes back to God's singling out of a particular tree that was forbidden. The question of 'Why?' – and hence 'Why not?' – was there from the beginning. It is as if God, like an over-protective father, had accidentally achieved the very thing He wanted to avoid. By trying to keep the children from the pain of knowledge, God led them to seek it; in trying to keep them in the Garden of Eden, in the paradise of childhood, God had given them the impetus to step outside – and once outside, there was no way back. When a certain innocence is lost, it cannot be recaptured, except by wilfully denying the new reality. It can only be rediscovered after a long journey through the new-found knowledge; and the journey of humanity, and of each individual person, is a quest to find that state of wholeness again outside the shelter of the garden.

So did they fall, or were they pushed? And is the 'Fall' the cataclysm that some theologies see it as – or is it a first, necessary step towards emancipation of humanity, the first liberation from the slavery of the womb? Because if it is only a 'fall' – then the journey back to God is either enmeshed in guilt, or so dependent on some external source of salvation that human creativity, generosity and goodness are reduced to mere irrelevances or successful strategies for a return to divine favour. But if it is a liberation, however bitter and painful it may be at the moment of separation, then human beings travel bearing a full responsibility for their life and their actions, for their choices and ultimately for their death. And, in terms of the biblical faith, they have also the ultimate freedom – to choose or not to choose God, and that in the end is what the adventure begun with Abraham is all about. The Rabbis expressed it with the saying, 'Everything is in the hands of heaven, except the fear of heaven.' Or, as Franz Rosenzweig expressed, 'Man should learn to trust in this freedom: to believe that, though he is limited in all forms of existence, he is totally free in his relationship to God.'

Perhaps it is the fear of that freedom that has led human beings so often to impose their own chains, often religious chains, upon themselves and others, rather than face the loneliness and demands such a challenge imposes. Because it is indeed a loneliness, as our Genesis text reminds us. For the eyes of the man and woman are opened, as the snake has promised, and what do they discover? That they are naked?

What does this nakedness mean? Again, we are the inheritors of a long tradition that explains this revelation in sexual terms, and the fig-leaf with which they seek to cover themselves becomes the mark of sexual fear and shame through which people have held each other in subjugation. Perhaps sexuality is what is meant – but it is not the first or most obvious meaning of the text. Because, if you look throughout the Bible at all the instances where different versions of the word *eyrumim* (nakedness) are used, its principal emphasis is something quite different. It is used of captives being taken away naked into slavery (Isa. 20.2–4); of the hero running naked from the field of battle on the day of defeat (Amos 2.16); of the helplessness

= helplessness

nakedness

of a child (Hos. 2.5) and the nakedness of a newly-born infant (Eccles. 5.14). Its primary sense is the helplessness and weakness of human beings. That is what they discovered when they ate the fruit and their eyes were opened and they saw for the first time their situation as God had already seen it, as God had tried to protect them from seeing it – that they were naked and helpless and dependent. That is the ironic conclusion to the snake's promise that they would be as God. And in fear and despair they try to cover their nakedness, because clothes give not only covering and protection, but also identity and significance to a person.

irony

This is not to discount entirely the sexual elements that may be here, but it is not the main point, as the biblical usage of the word clearly tells us. And it is the awareness of our helplessness as we leave paradise behind to face the world that gives us our dignity and magnificence, of all the creatures on earth, for we live with the knowledge of our death and the terribly narrow boundary that separates us from it. Yet even here we do not go unprotected. For though the fig-leaves Adam tries to wear do not seem very effective, God intervenes in the story to clothe the couple in clothes of animal skin. Perhaps somewhere behind this cryptic comment is a legend about the snake shedding its skin – but what must first affect us is the promise of God's protection for the couple at the very moment of their fall and departure. The clothes they make themselves are ineffective but not so the ones they receive from God. Again the paradox of that dual nature of human beings reappears in another guise – human frailty and divine protection, human realism and divine hope. It was expressed by the great Hasidic master, Nahman of Bratzlav:

> This entire world is but a narrow bridge, yet the essential thing is never to be afraid.

(127)

We cannot leave this story without a look at one other aspect, one perhaps even more potentially tragic in its implications than the expulsion from Eden. When Adam tries to hide from God, the latter asks him '*ayeka*', ('Where are you?'). This is not a request for information about his geographical location! Instead, as Rashi pointed out, it is an opening gambit for a conversation. It gives Adam the opportunity to admit what he has done and ask forgiveness from God for his disobedience.

literally

But Adam does not take the opportunity. He responds to God's question as if it was meant literally – 'I heard Your voice in the garden and I was afraid because I was naked and I hid'. When God asks him if he has eaten from the tree, Adam again passes up his chance and instead accuses the woman. And the woman in whom he was so pleased just a little time before, who was created to be his complement, his partner, becomes instead: 'The woman *you* gave to be with me, she gave it to me'; and this disloyalty and betrayal is to characterize so much of interpersonal behaviour throughout human existence.

This leads us into the second story I want to examine, because it, too, deals with life and death, but the central theme is another aspect of human existence. It is the tale of Cain and Abel, the sons of Adam and Eve; Abel the shepherd and Cain the worker of the land. We are given no more information about them till the moment Cain brings an offering to God of the fruit of the ground. Abel, too, brought the first-born of his sheep and the best parts of them. Though generations of Bible readers have tried to discern some difference between the two offerings – perhaps Cain gave any old fruit, while Abel gave the best – there is no real evidence of a difference.

We know that in some way God favours the offering of Abel, but not that of Cain. What this means or how it happens is not clear, though the Rabbinic exegesis noted that in both cases it is not the offering itself that God reacts to but to 'Abel and his offering' and 'Cain and his offering' – it is the person and his gift. Cain is angry and God gives him a warning in language that is a little obscure, but which seems to make some sort of sense to us. The Revised Standard Version (RSV) renders it: 'If you do well, will you not be accepted? And if you do not do well, sin is couching at the door; its desire is for you, but you must master it.' To what is the first phrase – 'if you do well' – related? Perhaps in the matter of sacrifice, if it is sincerely meant, or of good quality – though nothing in the text has yet suggested that Cain's sacrifice is at fault. The word translated as 'will you not be accepted' is an odd grammatical form of the verb *nasa* ('to lift up'), which sometimes is extended to mean to lift away, hence to remove, hence – in the matter of God's actions – to accept and forgive the sins of human beings. Presumably this lies behind the RSV translation.

The Jerusalem Bible, as does the New English Bible, in a footnote refers the 'lifting up' to Cain's face which has fallen, a sign of his anger or depression. That might clarify the image, but does not help our understanding a great deal. The most recent Jewish translation offers 'If you do well, there is uplift . . .', which at least preserves the fact that the 'lifting up' does not stand in relation to any particular word. The Jewish Bible scholar Umberto Cassuto relates this word to the opposite possibility that occurs in the second part of the sentence – of sin waiting at the door; and paraphrases: 'If you do well, you will be able to rise and stand firmly on your feet; but if not, the opposite will happen.' That is to say, the 'doing well' refers to Cain's response to God's non-acceptance of his offering.

It is to Martin Buber that we must go to find the implications of this spelt out, in a collection of essays on *Good and Evil*. 'What we have before us here', he writes, 'seems to me an example of that uncanny occurrence which the Scriptures themselves understand as divine temptation . . . The settlement beside the forbidden tree is also a temptation, but one which is *not* withstood, and another such is the disregard of Cain's offering.' He notes that, as with Adam and Eve, God enters into conversation with Cain and warns him about sin waiting for him. He continues:

> This is the first occurrence of the word, which is absent from the tale of the Fall, the word 'sin', and here it is apparently the name of a demon who, by nature a 'beast that lies in wait', at times lurks on watch at the entrance to a soul that does not intend good, to see if it will fall prey to him, that soul within whose power it still lies to overpower him. If the passage may be so understood, it is the truest example within the world's early epic literature of a divine being's appeal to men to decide for the 'good', that means to set out in the direction of the divine.[1]

In a way, says Buber, God is testing out what human beings do with the knowledge gained by eating of the tree of the knowledge of good and evil. For the journey back to that relationship with God that existed before can now only come out of the free choice of human beings to accept God's will over them. And in fact the rest of the Bible, starting with the call of Abraham, is the story of how this drama of God's search for those missing children, and the human quest for that restored relationship with God, is acted out on the stage of history. But suppose we strip the tale of its theology for a moment, what is it saying? That life is unfair, that there are no guarantees or certainties that what we do will receive the expected reward or punishment that we might like to happen. At least not in

---

[1] Martin Buber, *Good and Evil*, Scribner 1953, pp. 85ff.

an obvious and material way. Rather, whatever happens to us, whether positive or negative, is a challenge to us to seek within it, if we wish to, its potential for goodness and growth. This is not something that can be stated glibly or easily – in the face of the suffering that is the lot of most of humanity. This is not something that I feel qualified to state out of my own experience – but it is the lesson derived by people like Viktor Frankl and the artist Yehudah Bacon from the concentration camps. The latter expressed it as follows in a discussion I recorded with him many years ago:

It was much later that I really understood the meaning of suffering. It can have a meaning if it changes you for the better. As I learned from Martin Buber, the Hasidim say there are two forms of suffering: one has a positive influence and the other a negative. How do you tell the difference? Suffering from God teaches you something, and suffering from evil drags you down. Of course, at the time of suffering you don't see this. One of the greatest things it can teach us is a greater understanding of other human beings. It is so basic that it shakes you to your soul and therefore it shows you yourself and the reality of 'self' in other people – it opens your eyes to the reality of other human beings which you would never otherwise understand. Because of this you can come to understand even your oppressor. I don't say we have to learn understanding in this way, but it is one of the positive results of suffering.

The ultimate freedom to choose one's response is the theme of the psychiatrist Viktor Frankl:

We who lived in concentration camps can remember the men who walked through the huts comforting others, giving away their last piece of bread. They may have been few in number, but they offer sufficient proof that everything can be taken from a man but one thing: the last of the human freedoms – to choose one's attitude in any given set of circumstances, to choose one's own way. And there were always choices to make. Every day, every hour, offered the opportunity to make a decision, a decision which determined whether or not you could become the plaything of circumstance, renouncing freedom and dignity to become moulded into the form of the typical inmate.

I am sorry to bring here these dark images from the concentration camps. But Cain, the first murderer, and Abel, the first victim, are prototypes of the choices set before each of us in the face of his or her destiny, his or her frustration, his or her suffering. The testing of Cain by God becomes the model of all later tests in the Hebrew Bible which challenge the assumptions we make about God, the certainties we think contain the Eternal. We know this, even if we cannot at all times acknowledge it. The unknown prophet who speaks in the latter part of the book of Isaiah, perhaps wrestling with Babylonian beliefs that there are two powers acting in the world, the God of light and goodness and another power that is the source of evil, insists that God is a unity and must contain all powers. So he described God as the One who

> forms light and creates darkness
> makes peace and creates evil. (Isa. 45.7)

As a philosophical truth, we can cope with such an idea, but there are times when we cannot face it. In the Jewish morning service these words of Isaiah are quoted, but the Rabbis had the courage to make a small change. God is the one who

> forms light and creates darkness
> makes peace and creates *everything*.

The change from 'evil' to 'everything' is small – but it makes a safe space in which we can pray to God, who created us, with our good and our evil, and our ability to choose.

That seems to me to be the face of God that emerges from these early chapters of Genesis. The God who so loves his creation, human beings, that he allows them to experience the greatest gift, that of freedom to choose or not to choose God. That is not a very comfortable image, but it shows a deep respect for our humanity.

I fear that I cannot stop at this point without a further word of qualification. There is a particularly crude form of religious one-upmanship that tries to put down the image of God in the Old Testament as a God of anger and general nastiness at the expense of the God of the New Testament who is the God of love. The theory is patently absurd, as even the most casual reading of both Testaments will indicate. It is the God of the 'Old Testament' who first asks us to love our neighbour as ourselves, who describes himself as 'merciful and compassionate, patient and full of love'. One would hope that this need not be said but, of course, from time to time it does need to be said. And the idea that God tests human beings for their own good seems to be the theme of a number of the parables – the prodigal son, after all, is a re-working of the Cain and Abel story. So if we are not to fall into this trap and instead take seriously these two stories that we have examined, what does it teach us of the relationship between human beings and God in the beginning?

The Rabbis noticed a distinction between the description of God's relationship with Noah and with Abraham. Of Noah it says: 'He walked *with* God' (Gen. 6.9), but to Abraham God says: 'Walk *before* me . . .' (Gen. 17.1). What is the difference between these two statements, of walking *with* God or walking *before* God? The Rabbis said it is like a king who has two sons. To the child he says, 'Take my hand and walk with me'. But to the one who has grown up he says, 'Walk before me'! At times we need God to hold our hand and walk with us. At times, like a parent who respects the right of the child to grow up and gain its independence, we are grateful to be allowed, or even forced, to take the first faltering steps alone that are the expression of our independence and dignity. That seems to be why we had to leave Eden; and that is why Cain's offering was not accepted. That is why we are called to live out our lives in both the awesome fear and the wondrous love of God, as the Jewish prayer requests: 'Give us integrity to love and fear you – so shall we never lose our self-respect, nor be put to shame, for you are the power which works to save us.'

There is a telling reinforcement of this reading of the 'Fall' in the daily Jewish liturgy. In the *Amidah* 'the standing prayer', that is recited three times a day, there are three opening and closing blessings, but within them come thirteen others which represent the petitions that Jews lay before God, as one would before the king of an ancient court. The first of these is quite 'loaded' in its terminology when we think of the story we have just read.

You grace human beings with knowledge, and teach mortals understanding. Grace us with the knowledge, understanding and discernment that come from you. Blessed are you, Eternal, who graces (us) with knowledge.

The word for 'knowledge', repeated three times, is the same one as is used of the 'tree of *knowledge*', yet it is here described as being granted to us by God as an act of grace. I can think of no more telling proof of the Rabbinic view that far from being a 'fall from grace', the eating of the fruit and the subsequent expulsion from Eden, was ultimately a great liberation for it gave the 'children' in Eden the chance to grow up. God cut the strings of the puppets and let them walk erect upon the earth.

Perhaps the following prayer, also from the Jewish daily liturgy, is a further Rabbinic denial of any catastrophic effect of the 'fall' on the human soul. It recognizes the transience of our lives, but also the transience of death.

My God, the soul you have given me is pure, for you created it, you formed it and you made it live within me. You watch over it within me, but one day you will take it from me to everlasting life.

— 10 —

Are You Saved?

When European artists settled in Australia and began to paint the landscape, they painted the trees just the way they were back home. Actually they were quite different trees, but it took a long time before the artists could shake off their conditioning and see what was actually there. The same happens when people begin to meet in a dialogue situation. Each sees the other through the eyes of their own tradition and therefore asks questions based upon it. 'Do you also have . . .?' 'But how can you get to heaven if you don't . . .?' It takes a long time before we learn to hear the other properly and recognize the 'otherness' of their concerns, values, priorities. In terms of Jewish/Christian dialogue, although a lot of progress has been made in acknowledging the different agendas that both sides have, for most people still the old questions and assumptions are there. So it is worth while spending a little time looking at one such issue in some detail. As the title of this chapter suggests, it will be the vexed question of 'salvation'.

I find myself approaching this topic with great circumspection. In particular I want to avoid the risk of becoming apologetic. The term 'salvation' is deeply immersed in Christian theology and contains an emphasis that, if not foreign, is at least far less central to Jews. So part of me feels like saying, 'We've got salvation, too!' and another part wants to explore the Hebrew Bible without having to face at all the assumptions that a Christian environment forces us to bring to this subject.

Let me illustrate the problem by two examples. In preparing this chapter I looked up such biblical commentaries and theological works by Jews as I have readily available. I hoped to find a neat section in the index of each labelled 'Salvation' – and hardly ever found any such entry at all. Under 'Redemption' there is the odd remark, and under 'Messiah' there may be a lot to say, but the terminology of 'Salvation' is not one that enters into Jewish discussion with anything like the force that it has in Christianity and certainly without the particular overtones connected with the death and resurrection of Jesus of Nazareth.

The second illustration indicates the difficulty for a Jew in examining this topic when confronted with Christian approaches to it. As part of my preparation, I looked at the *Interpreter's Dictionary of the Bible*,[1] a very useful, wide-ranging encyclopedia that aims to provide an objective, scholarly evaluation of the various subjects it considers – certainly that has been my experience of it when I have consulted it before. But, when tackling the subject of salvation, examining it within both Testaments, that objectivity slips in peculiar, though to Jews all-too-familiar, ways. For example the author examines the question of whether the Hebrew terminology for salvation (based on the root *yesha*) refers to simple human acts of 'rescue' – i.e. non-theological usages of the term – and where does it move over into the area he terms 'salvation history': a view of the rescue of the particular hero as he plays his role in God's plan for the saving of the world?

He notes, quite rightly, that there are many cases in which it is not possible to make such clear-cut distinctions. He compares the stories of the adventures of the young David with 'the national sagas of many nations', and continues:

> They are not unlike the stories of Robin Hood and his Merry Men, beloved of children from generation to generation. Yet the David cycle is sacred history and the Robin Hood cycle is not. This is not because the stories about David are more edifying, more moral, than those about Robin Hood; indeed, in the matter of edification, there is little choice between the two cycles. The crucial difference between them is that the David stories belong to the line of God's action in the events of world history, which leads to the achievement of His purpose of the salvation of mankind. It was by a particular series of historical events, through a particular national history, that God's saving purpose in Jesus Christ was fulfilled. It is because salvation is in the name of Jesus Christ, and no other (Acts 4.12), that the biblical history is 'salvation history'; and it is for this reason that the salvation

[1]Keith Crim (ed.) *The Interpreters' Dictionary of the Bible*, 5 vols, Abingdon 1952, 1976.

story is the story of Abraham, Isaac, Jacob, Moses, Joshua, Rahab the harlot, Gideon, Barak, Samson, Jephtha, David, Samuel, and the prophets (Hebrews 11), not the story of Buddha, Confucius, Socrates, Plato, Artistotle, Marcus Aurelius, Plotinus, Mohammed, Rousseau, Marx, Gandhi, Bertrand Russell.

I think a number of elements must be isolated from that incredible statement. First, it is clear that he has imposed on to the Hebrew Bible a linear view of an unfolding salvation history leading to a clear-cut conclusion because of the emphasis on that view in the New Testament; that is to say he has imposed New Testament categories of thought on to the Old and, though Jews have had to put up with this for two thousand years, it is still shocking to hear it, and all the more so in a scholarly work on the Old Testament.

Secondly, the sheer exclusiveness of the claim to 'salvation history' and the suggestion that only the line through Israel (and hence Christianity) is legitimately recognized as such, is in direct contradiction to the universalism that frequently emerges in the Hebrew Bible – see the next chapter. One could certainly argue that the stories of Robin Hood, insofar as they reflect a concern with fighting injustice and asserting the rights of people to be free, conform to views held by the Bible, but the Bible itself contains references to people like Jethro, Melchizedek and Balaam, as we have already discussed above, who are clearly 'gentiles' who have both a recognition of the One God and contribute to Israel's wider understanding of the attributes of God. And the Persian king Cyrus had no small part to play as well, being called by the writer of the latter part of Isaiah 'God's servant'.

The Book of Jonah clearly makes a similar universal point, which probably indicates the degree to which there was a struggle within Israel itself to accept this broader reality. But Amos, who at first glance seems most preoccupied with internal Israelite problems, makes two wide-ranging statements about God's relationship to other nations. At the beginning of his book, he speaks of God's concern with the immorality of the surrounding nations, and how God will punish them, though that could also be seen as merely an appeal to the inner nationalistic pride of Israel. But the most explicit affirmation that 'sacred history' is to be seen and acknowledged within the secular history of other peoples is in Amos 9.7:

Are you not like the children of the Cushites to me, O Children of

Israel? says the Eternal. Did I not bring up Israel from Egypt and the Philistines from Caphtor and the Arameans from Kish?

That is to say, other nations have their 'Exodus from Egypt': that event – which as we shall see, is absolutely essential in Israel's self-understanding and the experience and working out of salvation – is also central to the lives of other peoples, and God was instrumental in bringing it about for them as well.

That there is a special task for Israel is equally clearly spelt out by Amos, for the Israelites were the first to respond in a conscious and collective way to God's offer of a covenant; and, because of this, very high expectations are put upon them in terms of their behaviour (Amos 3.2). But there is all the difference in the world between recognizing the unique task of a particular people alongside the universal significance and legitimacy of the journey of other peoples, and a narrow exclusiveness that is suggested in the commentary quoted above.

That final list of figures who do not count in 'salvation history' is in Jewish eyes just silly. It is, of course absurd – within a discussion of the Hebrew Bible – to put such a list together; it becomes pretty grotesque from any point of view to dismiss figures like Buddha, Socrates and Gandhi from the 'salvation history' of the world; and it clearly amounts to blasphemy from a Muslim point of view (and also a Jewish point of view, since Maimonides recognized the religious worth of Islam) to exclude Mohammed. In fact, the piece is so incredible that one wonders what is the underlying thought. That is revealed in the very next paragraph:

> Salvation history is the story of the divine action for our salvation in and through the lives and persons of real flesh-and-blood historical characters, as sensual and as fallible as men usually are, and yet who were, *through no virtue of their own* (my italics) made the instruments of the divine plan for the salvation of the world.

It is that phrase, 'through no virtue of their own', that separates this particular author's view of events from what, I would argue, is a more legitimate understanding of the position of the Hebrew Bible. Most obviously it is the qualities of Noah and Abraham that make God continue to work with human beings, and – in a remarkable reversal of its own conventions – it is the will and prayers of Hannah (I Sam. 1–2) that lead to the birth of Samuel and the ushering in of a new epoch. The very humanity of people like Jeremiah becomes an integral part of his teaching. In fact, such a view is so obviously untenable that it could only be asserted because of a very strong theological assumption made by the author that once again belongs to a particular sort of Christian viewpoint. This, too, is spelt out explicitly a little further on in the same article:

> After the profound theological insights of the Isaianic school had been achieved, the prophetic vision faded, and the great concept of salvation by the divine righteousness alone was obscured in the doctrines of later Judaism, especially those which implied salvation by works of human merit. According to the teaching of the Rabbis, the salvation of the individual was to be achieved by the meticulous observance of the detailed commandments of the Torah (law of Moses), and it was possible by a straightforward system of bookkeeping to ascertain a man's prospects of salvation by noting whether his merits exceeded his transgressions. Different schools of Rabbis awarded higher or lower points for this work of merit or that transgression, but all observed the same fundamental rules of the game. Moreover, it was generally agreed that a pious Jew who had tried, but had barely succeeded, might draw upon the bank of the superabundant merits of the fathers (Abraham, Isaac and Jacob) and of the Maccabean heroes. Salvation thus became largely a matter of human achievement assessed by the method of the balance sheet.
>
> Such was the nature of official (Rabbinic) Judaism at the end of the OT period and until AD 70; but, if we may judge from the evidence of the Qumran literature, the sect type of piety was little better. A fanatical legalism, which ordered a withdrawal from every kind of worldly contact, aimed at the salvation of a small community of the puritanically elect; the salvation which it envisaged was as far removed as possible from that which was proclaimed by Jesus to be available for publicans and sinners. Later Judaism knew only of salvation for the righteous and nothing of the salvation of sinners. It was Jesus and his followers, notably Paul, who undertook a reformation which consisted fundamentally in the rediscovery and assertion of the prophetic doctrine of salvation by the righteousness of God.

It is amazing that as late as 1962, when this was published, one can still find these parodies of Rabbinic Judaism trotted out as definitive statements. It clearly betrays a total ignorance of contemporary

Jewish writings and a very old-fashioned – let alone uncritical –
reading of the New Testament. To translate the word 'Torah' as
'law', without acknowledging that Rabbinic Judaism laid as much
stress on ethical, moral, spiritual, mystical and what one may term
'humanistic' values, is to distort the meaning of that word. In his
critique, the author ignores the concept of *teshuvah*, inadequately
translated as 'repentance', that offers a wide-open doorway to God.
One could go on, but I hope the point is made.

It is very difficult even to begin to talk of 'salvation' within the
context of the Hebrew Bible without immediately laying undue
emphasis on a subject that is implicit rather than explicit throughout, and without loading one's analysis with attempts to prove that
it does or does not stand up to what Christianity implies *should* be
there.

In what follows I will be putting emphasis on two elements that
are central to any discussion of salvation. The most obvious is the
Exodus from Egypt, which became not merely an account of a past
deliverance but also, through its liturgical usage, an ongoing
experience of the reality of salvation, and thus a model for
anticipating the future. The other is the story of Creation and the
image of a new creation, to be made by God, when disillusionment
has set in about the possibility of perfecting human society by the
actions of human beings alone. It is these two events that I would
like to examine in more detail, bearing in mind that there are other
approaches and aspects that could also be considered.

After four hundred years' silence, God speaks to Moses at the
burning bush. His speech, as is fitting for such a significant moment,
is constructed in a formal way using a concentric pattern.

> Then the Eternal said:
> I have surely *seen* the affliction of My people who are in Egypt,
> and have heard their *cry* because of their taskmasters;
> I know their pains.
>> I have come down to deliver them out of the hand of
>> Egypt and to bring them out of that *land*
>> to a *land* good and broad
>> to a *land* flowing with milk and honey
>> to the place of the Canaanites, the Hittites, the Amor-
>> ites, the Perizzites, the Hivites and the Jebusites.
> and now, behold, the *cry* of the Children of Israel has come to me,

and also I have *seen* the oppression with which the Egyptians oppress them.

Now come, I will send you to Pharaoh that you may bring out My people, the Children of Israel, from Egypt. (Ex. 3.7–11)

The structure is quite clear because of the repetition of certain key words. At the beginning, God says 'I have surely *'seen'* and at the end He again says 'I have *seen*' – the Hebrew root *ra'ah* being used both times. Moving in from this outermost ring, the key word is *tza'agah* (cry). In verse 7, God says He has heard their 'cry' and in verse 9 we learn that their 'cry' has come to him. This emphasis on God's awareness of the suffering of Israel is thus reinforced by the use of these two elements repeated in reverse order. The innermost part is built around the word *eretz* (land): God has come down to take them up from 'that land' of slavery to a land of freedom, one that is 'broad and wide', one that flows with milk and honey. Later in the same chapter, God will emphasize that he is fulfilling the promise he has made to the patriarchs, and there is considerable play on the revelation of God's name. But suppose we concentrate on this opening statement of intent.

The innermost part of the structure, and thus the part which is particularly emphasized, deals with the 'land', the leaving of *that* land (it is not even dignified with a name) which has come to symbolize all that is worst in human existence: slavery, cruelty, futile labour, callousness and, in the end, the ever-present threat of violent death. It is the exact opposite of the Garden of Eden, and it is no accident that the alternative that is offered is also a land spacious and fertile, a land promised by God to help fulfil the divine plan for the restoration of human beings – a land and a society which are to be the model of the new human community. Adam and Eve are barred from Eden because it contains the tree of life – but they and their offspring are equipped with knowledge and must find their way to a new Eden, one given by God, one which they must themselves make into a paradise.

It is worth noting two other themes related to the Exodus story that have wider consequences. The first is the issue of slavery and freedom. The first laws in the covenant law book given at Sinai (according to Ex. 21) deal with the rights of Israelite slaves to go free. The term used of the Egyptian treatment of the Israelites (*parekh* – rigour, harshness) only occurs in one other chapter in the Pentateuch, in Leviticus 25.43, which specifically commands that your own slaves should not be treated with *parekh*. Elsewhere it is only found in Ezekiel 34.4, where the prophet accuses the shepherds of the people of treating the Israelites with the same 'harshness' – the phrase here seemingly reflecting the earlier usage.

But it is not only the treatment of slaves that is examined. Four times the Israelites are called to remember that they were *gerim* (strangers, aliens) in the land of Egypt. For this reason they know the 'soul of the stranger': they should not oppress the stranger (Ex. 22.20; 23.9). In Leviticus 19, in a parallel to the famous phrase 'You shall love your neighbour as yourself' (Lev. 19.18), they are commanded to treat the resident alien as one born among them and to 'Love the stranger as yourself because you were strangers in Egypt, I am the Eternal your God' (cf. Deut. 10.19).

The repeated emphasis on this phrase in asserting the responsibilities of the new national existence of the people implies that concern for the outsider was not an automatic matter. Former slaves may use their new freedom to exert the same injustice on those in their power as they previously suffered themselves. Nevertheless, the command is there – Israelite society should be a model, not a regression to the slave state from which they had been liberated. Without that advance, the exodus would have been a futile exercise.

This emphasis on concern for other peoples, within the limited area of how one treated one's own resident foreign community, links up with another motif that runs through the exodus narrative: in particular the stories of the plagues. The theme begins with Pharaoh's assertion that he does not know the Eternal, Israel's God (Ex. 5.2). The implication of this use of the verb *yada* (to know) is not merely ignorance, but refusal to acknowledge either the existence or the authority of Israel's God. (The midrash has Pharaoh order his magicians to look up the name in the official record of all the gods in the world. When it is not there Pharaoh turns triumphantly to Moses, who replies: 'Do not look for the living God among the dead.') Ten times in the following chapters the verb *yada* recurs (7.5, 17; 8.6, 18; 9.14, 29; 10.2; 11.7; 14.4, 18), where it is emphasized that the latest plague, or the series as a whole, is so that Pharaoh, the Egyptian people and Israel itself, may *know* that God is the power behind these events. That is to say, the liberation of Israel from slavery is not merely an event of internal significance to Israel, but one which has consequences for the world at large.

In placing Israel on the world stage, so to speak, the power of

God is to be shown to all nations and, with that power, God's concern with those who suffer and his breaking of the yoke of servitude. It is for this reason that one of Moses' arguments when God threatens to destroy the people after the episode of the Golden Calf is to the appeal to God's reputation among the Egyptians who will say that God brought the Israelites out to kill them (Ex. 32.13). And similarly after the other major crisis, the episode of the spies, Moses not only refers to what Egypt might say, but also the nations of the land to which Israel is coming (Num. 14.13–16). There is more at stake in Israel's release from Egypt than its own salvation – there are lessons for the world.

With Egypt behind them, two destinations confront the newly released slaves: Sinai and the Promised Land. In God's second major speech in Exodus, also concentrically structured, a whole string of verbs spell out the stages of this process:

> I shall bring you out from under the burdens of Egypt
> and I shall rescue you from slavery to them;
> I shall redeem you with an outstretched arm and with great judgments;
> I shall take you to myself as a people,
> and I shall be your God;
> then you shall know that I am the Eternal your God who brings you out from under the burdens of Egypt
> and I shall bring you to the land which I raised my hand (in an oath) to give it to Abraham, to Isaac and to Jacob,
> and I shall give it to you as an inheritance.
> I am the Eternal. (Ex. 6.6–8)

'Redemption' here is the technical term for paying off the debts or otherwise acting to release someone from slavery, and the redeemer is the member of the family with that particular responsibility. God here acts in that manner to Israel and brings them into a covenant, a permanent contractual relationship, with mutual responsibilities. At Sinai, the implications of this are spelt out further. 'You shall be for me a kingdom of priests and a holy nation' (Ex. 19.6). As a priest becomes a mediator between the people and God, a normal human being with a specialized task, so Israel is to play the same role among the nations of the earth. In this intimate moment of decision, the outside world recedes, though even here it is stressed that God may choose Israel because 'all the world belongs to me'. That universalist background is never forgotten, and hence the widest implications of Israel's salvation from Egypt are linked up to the earliest promise made to Abraham, that through him all the families of the earth would be blessed (Gen. 12.3).

Intimately concerned with the Sinai revelation, of course, are the Ten Commandments – or the 'Ten Words' as they are known, perhaps more accurately, in Jewish tradition. Their exact relationship to the Sinai event is a highly complex matter, made more difficult by the recurrence of a version of this passage in Deuteronomy. Much play has been made, particularly in Rabbinic teaching about the *shabbat*, on the two different versions of the command to keep the sabbath day – an issue we have seen Ibn Ezra discussing in an earlier chapter. Yet the two reasons given for keeping the *shabbat* exactly reflect the two poles around which we have been examining the theme of salvation: Creation and the Exodus. The version in Exodus 20 enjoins Israel to remember the sabbath,

> because in six days the Eternal made the heavens and the earth, the sea and all that was in them, and rested on the seventh day, so the Eternal blessed the sabbath day and hallowed it (Ex. 20.11).

However, in Deuteronomy the reason for 'keeping' the *shabbat* is given as:

> You shall remember that you were slaves in the land of Egypt and the Eternal your God brought you out from there with a strong hand and with an outstretched arm, therefore the Eternal commanded you to keep the sabbath day (Deut. 5.15).

It is sometimes argued that whereas the Exodus version is a mere (*sic*) theological reason, the Deuteronomy one reflects a social concern and is thus of higher ethical value. The argument could also be reversed in that the emphasis on creation points to a more universal concept. But, be that as it may, it is fascinating that the theme of *shabbat* is underpinned by reference to these two events. They are linked again by that very word for 'slave' – *eved* – that has recurred through our discussion. For the same word which is used for the bitter servitude of Egypt is also the word used of the work that Adam himself did in the Garden of Eden when God placed him there 'to serve it' (Gen. 2.15).

Again, in the laws about the release of slaves in the jubilee year, the implications of all this are spelt out:

For (says God) it is to Me that the children of Israel are *avadim* (slaves/servants); they are My servants whom I brought out from the land of Egypt, I am the Eternal your God (Lev. 25.55).

No Israelite may be the slave of any other, for all belong to God. On *shabbat*, which is a taste in this unredeemed world of the perfect world that was the Garden of Eden, there are no slaves and human beings stand before God in their freedom. The state in which humans once stood in innocence as Adam, they can now attain through their own voluntary regulating of their society, and ultimately in their acknowledging of God as the creator of the universe and of themselves. Salvation, both as an internal and an external state, lies in the free choice of a free person and a free society to subsume their will to that of God – as expressed in part in the way they treat each other.

So powerful is the concept of freedom, and the insistence that the Israelite state be built on it, that the prophet Jeremiah sees the flouting of this principle as the ultimate crime for which there is no hope of forgiveness from God. In chapter 34 of his book there is recorded an event that took place during the siege of Jerusalem by Nebuchadnezzar. In response to Jeremiah's words, the princes of the people released slaves who should have been set free according to the sabbatical and jubilee laws. But when, at the approach of the Egyptian army, the Babylonians withdrew, the slaves were forcibly taken back again. Using the terminology of Leviticus 25.10 ('You shall proclaim liberty/release', *dror*) and of the legal passages in Exodus 21.2 (cf. Deut. 15.1–2), God condemns this corrupt breaking of the word. In punishment, God will in turn 'proclaim liberty' – to the sword, to the plague and to famine, as a punishment (Jer. 34.17). In view of this, it is not unexpected that the other major element that Jeremiah stresses as standing between Jerusalem and its occupation by foreign nations is the proper keeping of the sabbath (Jer. 17.19–27). For, ultimately, the keeping of *shabbat* is again the acknowledgment of God as creator, and the acceptance of God's will and plan for the saving of the world.

The implication that ultimately what happens within Israel has effects for the whole world is spelt out in the writings of Second Isaiah. It is fascinating to see yet again the keeping of the sabbath taking so prominent a part in the promise of salvation for all people – Israelite or foreigner (*nokhri*, one with no family ties to Israel at all):

Thus says the Eternal: Keep justice and do righteousness, for
soon my salvation will come and My deliverance be revealed.
Happy the person who does this, and the human being who holds
fast to it, who keeps the sabbath, not profaning it, and keeps his
hand from doing any evil. Let not the foreigner, who has joined
himself to the Eternal say: 'The Eternal will surely separate me
from his people', and let not the eunuch say: 'Behold, I am a dry
tree'. For thus says the Eternal: 'To the eunuchs who keep my
sabbaths, who choose the things I desire, and hold fast to my
covenant, I shall give them in my house and within my walls a
monument and a name better than sons and daughters; I will give
them an everlasting name which shall not be cut off. And the
foreigners who join themselves to the Eternal, to minister to him,
to love the name of the Eternal, and to his servants (*avadim*), all
who keep the sabbath and do not profane it and hold fast to my
covenant, these I will bring to my holy mountain, and make them
joyful in my house of prayer; their burnt-offerings and their
sacrifices will be accepted on my altar, for my house shall be
called a house of prayer for all peoples. (Isa. 56.1–7)

Whether through the agency of a human figure, the 'anointed
one', modelled on the image of the Davidic king; whether nations
shall flock to Zion to receive instruction in God's *Torah* and set
aside their weapons of war; whether there shall be fundamental
changes in nature such that animals of prey shall be in harmony with
each other and with human beings; whatever the specific imagery,
these visions of salvation for the world are concerned with the
establishment of justice and freedom for all under the reign of the
One God. It is the return to the harmony between human beings,
creation and God that was present in Eden, but this time brought
about through the desire of human beings themselves to help create
that harmony: the act, however unbalanced in terms of the
respective powers of human beings and God, must be one of
partnership and shared commitment. And, of course, it must be
open-ended.

   The experience of Israel is human experience in a human world,
subject to the infinite forms of social and political change. The
memory and the liturgical re-experiencing of the Exodus in the
Passover gave them a perspective and ultimately a vision, to carry
them through the second exodus from Babylon and on into the
second exile of Roman times. During the Festival of Tabernacles

(*Sukkot*), a total of seventy bulls was sacrificed, so this gesture was seen traditionally as being on behalf of the seventy nations of the world, indicating both Israel's responsibility for the world and the reality of the wandering in the wilderness that is life. Both festivals provide an eternal perspective against which the realities of daily existence of the individual and the nation could be evaluated. And the *shabbat*, with its regular reappearance after the six working days, becomes a model and a guarantor of the potential for salvation inherent in human will and human rest and surrender to the will of God. So salvation is both a promise of something to come and a present potential reality; it is a consolation in times of trouble and a challenge in times of prosperity and success.

In the liturgy for the sabbath day, there is an insertion into the standing prayer, the *Amidah*, specific to the day, and it manages to encapsulate within a few lines many of the themes we have discussed, seeing in the sabbath itself the model of the salvation that will come:

> Our God and God of our ancestors, may our rest be acceptable to you. Make us holy through doing your commands and give us our share in your *Torah*, your teaching. Satisfy us with your goodness and let our souls know the joy of your salvation. And purify our hearts to serve you in truth, and let us inherit, O Eternal our God, in love and favour, your holy sabbath, and may all Israel who make your name holy find in it their rest.

Salvation is God's gift to human beings, and, in no small way, it is a human gift to God.

—— 11 ——

Universalism and Particularism

Whether the Hebrew Bible is 'universalistic' or 'particularistic' is either not an issue at all, or else a burning question that demands serious discussion and evaluation. Obviously both elements, a strong nationalist identity of Israel, coupled with an awareness of Israel's God as the God of the entire world, are closely interlinked, if not ultimately inseparable. But their precise interrelationship and its consequences belong within a wider range of issues, both internal and external to Jewish self-understanding, and to the understanding of the Hebrew Bible by others, particularly the church.

Let me illustrate this with some examples of Jewish writing on biblical, and particularly, prophetic, universalistic ideas. The first is from a little book called *Highways through Judaism* by Rabbi Victor Reichert, an American Reform Rabbi and poet. It was published by the Soncino Press in Great Britain in 1936.

> That the Jewish people had lived creatively through centuries of dispersion and persecution is to be credited in no small part to the death-defying impulses set in motion by the spirit of the prophets. They gave Israel's religion a world outlook and a broad universalistic basis by envisioning a God who cared not only for Israel but for all mankind. Thus they freed the faith of the Jew forever from the fetters of a narrow, exclusive racialism and nationalism. The nameless prophet who wrote that little masterpiece, the Book of Jonah, taught the Brotherhood of Man to supplement and illustrate the prophetic doctrine of the Fatherhood of God. By identifying spirituality with the ethical life and the service of God with the service of man, the prophets prepared the way for that democratic, purified faith which could survive the shock of Israel's destruction (p. 17).

The sentiments expressed in this passage, such as the emphasis on universalism, the removal of 'the fetters of a narrow, exclusive racialism and nationalism', the teaching of the 'Brotherhood of Man' and a 'democratic, purified faith', are all comprehensible from Dr Reichert's background within classical American Reform Judaism. With its emphasis on finding a way for Jews to be full participants in American life while preserving the essential values of their tradition, with a deep concern with social issues as a way of expressing their adherence to the 'prophetic' aspects of Judaism, an American Reform Rabbi would quite naturally see such concerns as central to biblical prophetic teaching. Bearing in mind also that this book was written before the impact of the *Shoah* and the creation of the State of Israel, its openness and optimism of tone is further understandable.

However the following passage follows a similar line even though it dates from 1959, and comes from the pen of an orthodox Rabbi, an alumnus of Jews' College, the Orthodox seminary of Great Britain, and subsequently the lecturer there in Semitic Languages and Principal. Rabbi Dr Isidore Epstein, in a little Penguin paperback called simply *Judaism*, introduces his chapter on 'The Prophets' as follows:

> The faith to which Judaism owes its survival and dynamic is founded upon the Torah (Law) and the Prophets. The Torah, . . . communicates not only the ways of right conduct – religious and moral – but also the knowledge of God and of His Will. Fastening upon this knowledge, the prophets interpreted it with great force and freshness, leading thereby the religion of Israel into new paths through which it became the common inspiration of mankind. With them, as has been well remarked, developed a new interpretation of God, a new interpretation of man, and a new interpretation of religion. Thanks to their mighty strivings, monolatry blossomed into monotheism, nationalism into universalism, and religion became a matter of righteous living rather than mere ritual practice (p. 55).

A little further on he contrasts Hebrew and Greek views:

> And not for Israel alone was this future foreseen. While the prophets held fast to their national consciousness, their conception of history was that of world-history. Greek philosophy may have enriched by its speculations the conception of the soul of the

individual man, but it gave no thought to the individuality of peoples other than the Greeks. The barbarians, the name whereby they designated all foreign peoples, did not enter the horizon of Greek philosophy. The prophets of Israel, on the other hand, rose above the boundaries of their own nation to a vision of a unified humanity, and made the conception of mankind a content of religion. They had a vision of a world unity and harmony in which all men and peoples acknowledge and reverence God, the Lord of all the earth' (p. 59).

In both these writers, with their strong emphasis on universalistic values, there seem to be echoes of an apologetic stance made necessary for Jews by Christian evaluations of Judaism. The particular aspect of this that affects biblical scholarship is summarized by Yehezkel Kaufmann in his monumental four-volume Hebrew *History of the Religion of Israel*.

Christian doctrine regards the destruction of Jerusalem as merited by the continuous sin of Israel, which was climaxed by the rejection of Jesus. Israel's sinfulness, rooted in a constitutional tendency to rebellion, led ultimately to its being rejected by God. Whether consciously or not, this conception underlies the modern interpretation of Israelite history which has been formulated by Christian scholars. It is reflected in the scholarly axiom that the Israelite people was pagan, only the prophets and their circles transmitting the monotheistic idea. The god of the popular religion is described as a syncretistic YHWH-Baal, naturally connected with the people and the land. It was therefore necessary that Israel undergo a violent deracination in order to be sundered from its old territorial-natural religion. National collapse and exile was the precondition for the victory of prophetic monotheism over popular beliefs. It was consequently the inner demand and ultimate object of prophecy, although to be sure the prophets as individuals loved their people. In the prophecy of the fall adequate expression was finally given to the radical opposition between the particularistic, syncretistic faith of the people and the universalistic monotheism of the prophets. In the flames of his temple the god of the popular religion perished; the destruction was the victory of prophecy. In Second Temple times Judaism again became 'national', and prophetic universalism was again opposed by the national particularism of the folk; the old struggle was renewed.[1]

This part of Kaufmann's work first appeared in 1948 in Hebrew. Since then there has been a re-evaluation of the presuppositions of biblical scholars in their approach to the Hebrew Bible, or, rather, new methods of approaching the text have shifted the emphasis away from historical-critical methods. But as recently as 1984, Joseph Blenkinsopp in an evaluation of 'Old Testament Theology', can plead for a shift in perspective that would

> restate the standard antitheses – Christian universalism over against Jewish particularism, Christian freedom from the law over against Jewish legalism, etc. – as issues *internal to Judaism* on which different positions could be taken, and in fact were taken, during this entire period.[2]

Is it possible to get out of the apologetic mould in trying to evaluate the relationship of Universalism and Particularism in biblical thought? An attempt is made by Professor Harry Orlinsky in an article whose title indicates the distinction he is trying to make: 'Nationalism-Universalism and Internationalism in Ancient Israel'.[3] There is a somewhat testy tone to his writing that suggests that he has been exposed to too many 'universalistic' sermons by Reform rabbinical colleagues and graduates of the Hebrew Union College where he has lectured. In his popular book *Ancient Israel* (Cornell University Press 1954) he writes of the problem as follows:

> Another, and perhaps the most important of the concepts anachronistically read back into the tradition of the prophets was the idea that their teachings broadened out until they encompassed all humanity in a common brotherhood. One of the most frequently quoted, and erroneously interpreted, Bible texts is the well-known passage from Malachi: 'Have we not all one father? Has not one God created us?' (2.10). But this verse has been

---

[1]Yehezkel Kaufmann, *The Religion of Israel*, trans. and abridged by Moshe Greenberg, Allen & Unwin 1961, p. 403.

[2]Joseph Blenkinsopp, 'Old Testament Theology and the Jewish-Christian Connection', *JSOT* 28, 1984, pp. 3–15, p. 12. That we are still a long way from a general re-evaluation of standard Christian views on Judaism is evident from such books as *Anti-Judaism in Christian Theology* by the late Dr Charlotte Klein (SPCK 1978).

[3]In *Translating and Understanding the Old Testament*: Essays in Honour of Herbert Gordon May, ed. H. T. Frank and W. L. Reed, Abingdon Press 1970, pp. 206–36.

wrenched violently out of its original context when it is made to refer to all mankind . . . The prophetic tradition rests squarely on the idea of the Covenant between the Lord and His people Israel. The prophets were concerned directly and exclusively with this 'chosen people', and they took notice of other peoples and nations only when the latter came into contact – invariably for bad rather than good – with Judah and Israel. 'Hear this word that the Lord has spoken concerning you', Amos said. 'You only, have I recognized of all the families of this earth' (3.1–2). The concept of equality between nations would have been incomprehensible to the prophets or their people. It was an idea that could develop only later and under wholly different circumstances and which, not surprisingly, was read back into the prophetic texts by both Jews and Christians when Rome forced the Jews into exile after AD 70 and they found themselves adrift in the vast reaches of the Empire (pp. 163f.).

He continues by pointing out that the land of Israel was situated at the military crossroads of the Ancient Near East. Israel lived in constant fear of her neighbours like Assyria, Aram, Egypt and Babylonia. Their one desire was to be left alone, and 'it was this overwhelming desire that Isaiah (2.4) and Micah (4.3) expressed in the famous lines:

> And (the Eternal) shall judge between the nations,
>   and shall decide for many peoples;
> And they shall beat their swords into ploughshares,
>   and their spears into pruning hooks.
> Nation shall not lift up sword against nation,
> neither shall they learn war any more.'

He continues:

> Read wishfully, this majestic passage might be construed, as it so often has, to imply a desire for the brotherhood of men and universal peace on earth. In hard fact, the context excludes this sentimental interpretation (p. 165).

Orlinsky does accept that in the prophetic view the gentile nations would eventually come to realise that 'Israel and her religion and her God and His abode on Zion – that these constituted the only proper way of life in the entire world. The gentile peoples of the world would then come streaming to the mountain of the Lord's house' (pp. 166f.).

To summarize Orlinsky's views:

> To the biblical writers, from first to last, God is not only Israel's God alone, exactly as Israel is God's people alone, but he is at the same time, and naturally so, also the God of the universe, the only God in existence in the whole world, the only God who ever existed and who will ever exist . . . And so, the God of Israel is at the same time the sole God and Master of the universe without being the God of any nation but Israel: the *national* God of biblical Israel is a *universal* God, but not an *international* God. With no people other than Israel did God ever enter into a legally binding relationship (pp. 213f.).

A similar view is expressed by Martin Buber in comparing Amos 2.10 and 9.7. 'Amos' saying about the bringing up of the Arameans disposes of such a notion: 'the people do not know who is their liberator, they each call him by a different name, each one thinks to have one of its own, whereas we know the One, because He "has known" us. This is the *national* universalism of the prophetic faith.'[4]

In the end Orlinsky's insistence sounds almost like an anti-apologetic apologetic, though he argues well with the particular cases he cites. However, there are a number of passages within the Hebrew Bible that make such clear distinctions a bit more ambiguous. Most obviously, if we view the Bible as a whole, because of its beginning with the book of Genesis. The assertion of a single God, creator of heaven and earth and of a single man from whom all the rest of mankind descend are both revolutionary views, the latter flying in the face of obvious differences of race, language and nationality. The equation of one God and one mankind is now a given because of the widespread influence of the biblical view. So much so that we (at least in our corner of the West) consider racism as an aberration. Yet it is so deeply unacceptable, contravening 'common sense', national, cultural, religious and tribal loyalties, that prejudice against 'the other' continually leads to outbreaks of violence, on local and even global scales. Nevertheless the placing of Genesis at the beginning of the Bible puts the history of the patriarchs, the tribes, and the Israelite nation itself, on a stage of a

[4]Martin Buber, 'Holy Event' in *Biblical Humanism*, London 1968, pp. 63–79, p. 66.

world of nations and peoples, created by a sovereign God. Their chosenness is always set against this perspective; their successes and failures, their relationship to the land, never exist in a vacuum, however parochial the immediate view may seem to be of the individual book or writer. However early or late we date the book itself, or the individual parts, even if we limit ourselves to considering the process of canonization whereby the decision was made to place it there, it is an astonishing assertion of the significance and role of Israel and suggests an awesome temerity or conviction.

The metaphor for the relationship between God and the creation as well as between God and Israel is that of a series of covenants, contractual commitments with obligations binding upon both partners. Raphael Loewe[5] describes them as a series of concentric circles. 'The divine plan unfolds itself in a series of covenants, either explicit or implicit, established or imposed upon a series of contracting concentric circles: beginning with the cosmos . . ., and proceeding *via* Noah (i.e. humanity in general) through Abraham, to Israel. Within the "Israel" circle fall two others, not concentrically arranged, *viz.* the covenant with the Aaronic priesthood and that with the Davidic dynasty. These, however, are not to be regarded as a further restriction of the human contracting party . . .'

It is to this metaphor, clearly deeply embedded by then in Israel's self-consciousness as a nation, that Jeremiah can refer when he speaks of a new, or renewed covenant with Israel after the destruction he sees as coming (Jer. 31.31ff.). Similarly the prophetic voice of Isaiah 42.6 (49.8) can speak of God's servant becoming a 'covenant of peoples', an obscure phrase that nevertheless sees a central role for Israel in the salvation of all peoples. Clearly, along with Orlinsky, the implication here is that nations, recognizing God's deeds with his special people Israel, will come to worship him alone, even joining themselves to Israel and serving them in the process – but there is also a direct responsibility of Israel to the nations, a relatedness to them that must also be noted. Otherwise how are we to understand the repeated demand that Israel are God's witnesses whose task is to take to heart what they have themselves experienced of God's power (Isa. 43.10–12) and make it known to the peoples (Isa. 55.4).

[5]'Potentialities and Limitations of Universalism in the *Halakhah*' in *Studies in Rationalism, Judaism and Universalism in Memory of Leon Roth*, ed. Raphael Loewe, London 1966, pp. 115–50, p. 118.

A witness, presumably, has to testify, but does this mean active engagement with others, leading to a concept of mission, or is Israel's mere existence, and the fulfilment of its internal convenantal obligations, sufficient? Into this question should be added the terminology of 'blessing', that accompanies the call of Abraham, taking us back once more to Genesis. In Genesis 12.3 God promises Abraham: 'I will bless those who bless you, and curse those who curse you; and through you shall bless themselves all the families on the earth.' E. A. Speiser in his commentary on Genesis notes the difficulty with this latter phrase:

> The Hebrew form is often translated as 'shall be blessed', inasmuch as it is Niphal, which is generally, though not always, passive. There are however, parallel passages with the Hithpael (see xxii 18, xxvi 4), a form that can be reflexive or reciprocal, but not passive. What the clause means, therefore, is that the nations of the world will point to Abraham as their ideal, either in blessing themselves (Dr.), or one another (Ehrl.). The passive, on the other hand, would imply that the privileges to be enjoyed by Abraham and his descendants shall be extended to other nations.[6]

However neither translation would convey the meaning of the identical grammatical form as it occurs in Jeremiah 4.2: 'If you (Israel) swear "as the Lord lives" in truth, in justice and in uprightness, then nations shall bless themselves in Him and in Him shall they glory'.

Thus Benno Jacob sees Genesis 12.3 as leading to a different implication.

> *And by you all the families on the earth shall bless themselves* or 'be blessed'. Both translations are possible. The first would mean that all people will say among themselves of Abraham, would that our people be blessed like him. The second would mean: all peoples will be blessed through you as a consequence of their relation to you, even if they do not recognize the true relationship of cause and effect. This blessing is repeated when Abraham shows himself as an example of moral and religious greatness (18.18 and 22.18).[7]

[6]E. A. Speiser, *Genesis*, Anchor Bible, Doubleday 1962, p. 86.
[7]Benno Jacob, *The First Book of the Bible Genesis*. His commentary abridged, edited and translated by E. I. Jacob and W. Jacob, Ktav 1974, pp. 86f.

In the case of Abraham's intervention for the people of Sodom and Gomorrah (where the blessing formula is repeated) it is precisely the latter view that is exemplified. Furthermore, Abraham as an intercessor with God on behalf of King Abimelech (Gen. 20.17) cures the barrenness of Abimelech's wives so that they bear children, the most tangible 'blessing' available to Israelite society. That is to say, from Israel's founder to one of her latest prophets Israel's relationship with God, does not stand in the way of an engagement with, sometimes for and often against, the surrounding nations. Even if, following Orlinsky, in the passages where the prophets condemn the surrounding nations it is Israel who is addressed and not those nations themselves, nevertheless they express at the very least an international concern and consciousness, and perhaps an almost magical belief that the power of the words themselves has a tangible effect.

But is the world in biblical consciousness rigidly divided into Israel that 'knows' God and the rest of the world that does not? Clearly a number of people come, as individuals, to recognize Israel's God and associate themselves with him in some way or other. Most obvious is Ruth, or people like Na'aman, commander of the army of the King of Syria (II Kings 5), who acknowledged Israel's God when his leprosy was cured. Yet figures like Melchizedek, Balaam and to some extent Jethro, are 'outsiders' whose perception of the one true God is in some way similar to that of Israel. They are exceptional figures, as is that other non-Israelite champion of God, Job, nevertheless their existence and significance is confirmed. That even entire nations, or superpowers in this case, can share Israel's relationship with God while retaining their own identity is the view of one passage from the Book of Isaiah, however late it must be dated:

> In that day shall Israel be the third with Egypt and with Assyria, a blessing in the midst of the earth; for that the Eternal of hosts has blessed him saying 'Blessed be Egypt my people, and Assyria the work of my hands, and Israel my inheritance' (Isa. 19.24–25).

Perhaps the two options for the nations *viz.* joining themselves to Israel or accepting God while maintaining their own identity, is best expressed in the Book of Jonah which is usually cited in relation to Israel's particularism or universalism. The only point to make here is that Jonah encounters two groups of people, the sailors and the

Ninevites. Both are led to an experience of divine power and favour through the unwitting or unwilling activity of the prophet. But whereas the sailors will in the end call upon YHWH, Israel's God and vow to him vows and offer sacrifices (Jonah 1.14–16), the Ninevites, through the person of their king, will still call out to 'God' (Jonah 3.8) in the hope that 'the God' will turn back from his anger. Even though the king is quoting Jeremiah's theology, he is still not speaking to Israel's God by name, and indeed it is 'the God' who relents and does not destroy Nineveh. Since the particular designations of God within the book play an important role, we must recognize here a deliberate distinction. Whatever the subsequent fate of Nineveh, it is the universal God they are addressing as far as their limited consciousness will allow.

How far do these various theological reflections of Israel relate to the reality of Israel's experience with other nations. Whatever historical view one takes of Israel's origins, the experience within and with Egypt was clearly perceived as shaping the nation's initial identity. The Canaanites, whether as individual nations or as a collectivity, were the indigenous population among whom they dwelt, with whom they warred, entered uneasy alliances and subdued. There was interaction on private and public levels, intermarriages, mutual political and religious influence. The ever-changing borders led to continual reassessment of their immediate neighbouring countries, whether as foes, allies, vassals or conquerors. From the time of David and Solomon, Israel was open to the widest possible experience of the cultures of the known world, a crossroads and marketplace for every fashion of the time, be it in ideas, religion, technology or merchandise. And beyond the immediate borders, the great powers would also intrude, whether passing through to fight each other, or to stake their claim on that same little coastal strip. Solomon could express the meaning of this reality in terms both political and religious, for the two are closely interlinked, in his prayer at the inauguration of the Temple.

> Likewise when a foreigner, who is not of your people Israel, comes from a far country for the sake of your name (for they shall hear of your great name, and your mighty hand, and of your outstretched arm), when he comes and prays toward this house, hear in heaven your dwelling place, and do according to all for which the foreigner calls to you; in order that all the peoples of the earth may know your name and fear you, as do your people

Israel, and that they may know that this house which I have built is called by your name (I Kings 8.41–43).

And Israel was to experience exile in Babylon, in the heart of an alien Empire. In anticipation of the consequences of this, the prophet Jeremiah could formulate a command for the exiles that represents perhaps the exact converse of the experience of Solomon, yet further defines the relatedness of Israel to the outside world.

Thus says the Lord of hosts, the God of Israel, to all the exiles whom I have sent into exile from Jerusalem to Babylon: Build houses and live in them; plant gardens and eat their produce. Take wives and have sons and daughters; take wives for your sons, and give your daughters in marriage, that they may bear sons and daughters; multiply there, and do not decrease. But seek the welfare of the city where I have sent you into exile, and pray to the Lord on its behalf, for in its welfare you will find your welfare (Jer. 29.4–7).

For this insight Jeremiah was branded a traitor to his people. Yet the much-maligned Book of Esther confirms the truth of his perception. Beneath its surface fantasy, is the most realistic account of the situation of Israel in exile, a pawn in alien power politics, surviving as best it can by mastering the same political skills. From the listing of the nations of the earth that descended from the sons of Noah (Genesis 10) to the temporary success in the capital of a Persian Empire that ruled over one hundred and twenty-seven provinces, Israel knew and interacted with all aspects of the outside world. That reality cannot be reduced to a few limited theological principles. Rather one must recognize the consequences and polarization implied in that statement about Israel's destiny that accompanied the entry into that first covenant with God at Sinai; to be a kingdom of priests and a holy nation. Priests act as intercessors between the people, here the peoples of the world, and God; but a 'holy nation' means a nation set apart, different and other. To be within the world yet not of the world, both at the same time. Like their invisible God of history, Israel must be both immanent and transcendent, and ever suffer the pain of that irreconcilable polarization.

I began with the problem of apologetics, and with it I must end. Biblical law recognized two special categories of foreigner toward whom Israel had a special responsibility because they lived in

Israel's territory and came under Israelite law. The *ger*, though from another nation, was a permanent resident in Israelite society and had rights, both political and religious, in many areas equal with those of the Israelites. The *nokhri* was a foreigner whose stay was temporary, and the term acquired negative connotations, associated with the idolatrous practices of other nations. When Ruth emphasized her astonishment at Boaz's kind treatment of her, even though she was a *nokhriah* (2.10), the alienness of the term is being emphasized. If biblical Israel is no more, nevertheless the question of who belongs to Israel, how Israel relates to its neighbours and foreign citizens, what constitutes the boundaries of Israel's territory, real and ideal, are burning issues since the re-emergence of the State. And though Rabbinic law has long since superseded biblical law, and in turn been partly superseded by the secular legal systems of the powers that have ruled Palestine over the centuries, nevertheless it is back to the Bible that some are turning to tackle these and related issues. The territorial question of what constitutes the land of Israel in biblical times cannot be answered, because different strands of tradition give utterly different pictures, the whole being further coloured by classical Rabbinical views.[8] Which means that in the end the decision made by a person or group is largely subjective, the texts and arguments being marshalled to prove a given point, be it maximalist or minimalist. No less subjective and arbitrary are the attitudes to resident Arab populations within the pre-1967 borders, the occupied territories and the surrounding countries. If it is the most extremist views that get the greatest coverage in the media they nevertheless reflect one end of a broad spectrum of views that must have existed in biblical times as well. As indeed do the views of the surrounding nations to the new Israeli State mirror actions and attitudes of the biblical Israel's neighbours. The *real-politik* and the religious interpretations are once again, as then, hopelessly intertwined. The particularism or universalism of biblical Israel are no longer of merely academic interest, they are out in the marketplace and the political arena.

If there is no simple solution to any of these issues, or any objective point on which to fasten from the biblical record, nevertheless there are two statements in the Book of Leviticus, the priestly book of the 'kingdom of priests', that put them into perspective. 'The land shall not be sold in perpetuity, for the land is

[8]Moses Aberbach, 'The Boundaries of Israel', *Midstream*, May 1984, vol. 30 no. 5, pp. 13–18.

mine (says the Eternal); for you are strangers and settlers with me' (Lev. 25.23). 'For to me the children of Israel are servants, they are my servants whom I brought forth out of the Land of Egypt; I am the Eternal your God' (Lev. 25.25). It is as servants of the Eternal that Israel acquires its identity; it is by acknowledging that the land belongs to the Eternal that Israel is allowed to inherit it. And both of these hold true because of the words of the Psalm: 'The whole earth is the Eternal's and the fullness thereof, the world and those who dwell therein' (Ps. 24.1).

— 12 —

Prophets in Conflict

There is no shortcut into the world of the biblical prophets. On the level of narrative, the tales of wonder-workers, of loyal servants of God taking a stand against the kings, priests and people of their time, of seers who can see into the future, of wandering bands of ecstatics, on this level we can relate to their stories as we have done from our childhood. Elijah confronting the prophets of Baal and pouring water on the altar before the flame from heaven sets it alight; Jonah asleep in the bottom of the ship while the storm rages around him; Moses, the father of the prophets, brandishing the Ten Commandments before smashing them, or praying to God on behalf of his errant people; Jeremiah on the steps of the Temple threatened by an angry mob because he dared to suggest that Jerusalem might fall; perhaps Ezekiel eating the scroll with the words of God, or Isaiah standing before the throne of God in his vision, his lips purified by a burning coal.

As figures of mystery, of a strange power in direct communication with God; or even as individuals tortured by the message of destruction they must bring to the people and the land they love, they grip us and hold us. They are the outsiders who cannot conform to the corrupt norms of their society, people of such sensitivity that the little compromises we make in our everyday life appear to them as enormous sins, creating vast walls between us and our God.

All these images, and indeed many more, are true, at least on the level of myth or legend or projection. It is when we attempt to come to grips with the reality behind them, both in its historical aspect and in terms of the body of literature they left behind, that problems emerge. It is a platitude to suggest that the more we know the deeper the mystery becomes. But in this case with greater knowledge comes not only greater wonder together with recognizable human contradictions and features, but also an overwhelming sense of frustration at the things that cannot be fathomed because the language, the context, the very nature of the culture that gave birth to the prophets, is too often beyond our powers of reconstruction. Worse still, the understanding we obtain is too often only a construct, however scientifically researched, that reflects our own transient presuppositions, to be replaced within a few years by another fashionable artefact. We remake the prophets time and again in our own image – that is their power and that is a reflection of their inevitable failure.

The problems we face as historians evaluating the Bible are enormous because our only direct witness is the Hebrew Bible itself which is such a mixture of materials with so many different concepts of truth or reality at play within it that it is hard to extract 'verifiable data'. Yet at the same time the Bible sometimes expresses concern with locating particular events within their historical context, at least on an editorial level. The patriarchal stories and the various narratives up to the events described within the Book of Kings seem to us legendary in character, telling as much about the cultural or political forces behind the editing as they do about the events they describe – though this is also a reflection of the nature of our own historical enquiry. But with the classical prophets we often find detailed attempts to record the names of witnesses to key events. It seems to have been a matter of some concern to testify as to the precise moment that something took place or something was said, in advance of the series of catastrophes culminating in destruction and exile which the prophets predicted and to which they were sometimes witnesses.

The biblical reading and recording of its own history is no more, nor any less, subjective than ours. It too worked within a framework of certain presuppositions about what was important to preserve, record and teach. Whether we look for economic forces at work in the history of a civilization, or for the hand of God, we have consciously attempted to organize our information around an ideological construct. The ability of the biblical record to put on trial the whole of its own culture, to examine with shocking honesty its failures, that historical quest and presentation is in itself a tribute to the influence of the prophetic quest to see the world of the everyday through the eyes of an eternal God.

As historians we seek the origins and development of this phenomenon. To begin with the language itself, we have a number of terms that may or may not be identified with each other. The *ro'eh*, the 'seer', the *hozeh*, 'the visionary' seem to testify to figures that dreamed dreams or saw visions, perhaps able to look into the future – though the etymology of words may not tell us what the term came to mean in its later usage. The *ish ha-elohim*, the 'man of God', may be associated with miracle-working events; whereas the *navi*, possibly meaning 'messenger', points to a divine mission, and perhaps an emphasis on the 'word' that comes directly from God. Yet the term *navi* can cover such widely differing figures as Abraham and Moses of a far earlier period, the ecstatic dancing figures that Saul met after being anointed by Samuel, and the subtle poets and refined intellectuals like Isaiah or Jeremiah.

Their origins are obscure, with equivalent figures, but not exact counterparts, in the ancient near East. Abraham is a *navi* – but is that an anachronistic reading back into the past of the term or does it refer to his specific function as an intercessor with God on behalf of another as he does in the court of Abimelech (Gen. 20.7)? Moses is *par excellence* the *navi*, and he is the one who expresses the hope that all Israelites should be prophets (Num. 11.29). But is this a genuine historical reminiscence or part of a tradition belonging to prophetic circles that ascribes the origins of the profession to the great leader of the people, just as the priesthood is traced back to his brother Aaron? We hear in earlier passages of other occasional individuals who are prophets, notably Miriam and Deborah, but the phenomenon seems to be established in a more organized way at about the same time as the monarchy begins. If one may move from a historical to a more cultural perspective, there seems to be a recognizable change in significance with the appearance of Samuel.

Samuel, the leader saviour whose birth was the response of God to the prayer of his mother Hannah, is a transitional figure at a crucial moment in Israelite history. The different tribes had led their independent existence, coming together in loose alliances, continually under threat from neighbouring nations. According to the religiously structured history of the Book of Judges, at moments of disaster the people turned back to God who sent help in the form of leaders, variously understood to be chieftains or judges, who could briefly unite local tribal groups to fight off the enemy. During the lifetime of such a leader peace was maintained, but with his or her death the people again strayed from their God, to be punished again by an enemy as the cycle repeated itself. Samuel was the last of these judges or rulers at a time when the threat of invasion led to the political recognition that the emergent nation needed a greater unity personified in the figure of a king – like all the surrounding peoples. Samuel was opposed to this, seeing in the desire for a king a reliance on the conventional values of millitary strength rather than trust in God, and perhaps worried about the semi-divine identity given to kings in the surrounding culture. In the event he must yield to *realpolitik* and is responsible for anointing in succession the ill-fated Saul and the triumphant David. It is in the comparison of these three figures that one perspective on the role of the prophets emerges.

Samuel contained within his person three major functions. He was a priest at the sanctuary at Shiloh and performed sacrifices at local shrines on his journeys round the land. As judge he was effectively a political leader and in fact in trying to set up his sons as his successors was himself entering the delicate area of the establishing of hereditary authority over the people. Till now such a procedure had been resisted, either by the ruler himself, such as Gideon, or by divine action as in the case of Eli, the priest, Samuel's predecessor at Shiloh. Samuel was also called a 'seer' which, the text informs us, is the earlier term for a *navi*, a prophet. He is thus 'king', 'priest' and 'prophet' all at once, a combined role only previously played by Moses.

With Saul it is possible to trace an attempt to maintain all three powers in the same way. Thus Saul at the outset joins the band of ecstatics, becomes the first king and will attempt to make sacrifices. In all three actions he proves a failure. From his ecstatic experience no message seems to come, and the 'spirit of God' that rests upon him will later abandon him. As a 'priest' his sacrifices are either mistimed or interrupted and never completed. And as king, despite heroic moments and a death of great dignity, he proves to be too arbitrary and too weak to lead the people, disclaiming responsibility for their actions when confronted by Samuel. The contrast with David is fascinating. From early on in his guerilla days he takes with him a priest, Abiathar, one of the survivors of the priests of Nob slain by Saul (I Sam. 22.20–23). Later he is joined by a succession of people who are to become court prophets, most notably Nathan who rebukes him in the matter of Bathsheba (II Sam. 12).

It is as if David has delegated the two functions of priest and prophet to others, retaining for himself only the kingship, and thus by separating these powers, creating a series of checks and balances within the leadership of the Israelite society. The king is the anointed one of God, he has a formal religious role, but his power lies within the wider political area. The cult, with its regulative function in holding the balance of energies within the cosmos, of sustaining the eternal cycles of festivals and rituals that underlie the relationship between Israel and its God, is firmly in the hands of the priesthood. And acting as a sort of safety valve to modify that relationship with God according to the changing demands of everyday reality stands the prophet, the spokesman of God who warns and corrects the people, and the representative of the people who pleads their cause before God.

The historical pattern behind this division of authority may not be traceable, but what is clear is that by the time of the established monarchy there is also an established and organized prophetic tradition and office. They have a special jargon evidenced by the formulae and vocabulary of their speeches; they appear regularly in the framework of the court, their knowledge of God's will being sought by the king. And like all establishment functionaries, they seem to fall into the trap of becoming maintainers of the *status quo*, automatic confirmers of royal policies and uncritical accepters of the religious state of their society.

From their ranks step a few extraordinary figures who are *the* prophets of biblical tradition, for whom the word of God was a call to step outside convention and convenience and witness to a harsher truth.

By stressing their origin within a living tradition we are reminded that there is a framework within which they worked. Their language owes its forms to that tradition even when, as with Amos, they appear to disown their relationship to it. In his assertion that he is neither a prophet nor the son of a prophet (Amos 7.14), it is assumed that Amos is saying that he is not, so to speak, professionally trained, but was specifically called out from his daily occupation by the overwhelming effect of the word of God, something that could similarly happen to anyone. However, his description of the visions he received, his stepping in to plead with God for Israel's survival, his very language, seem to depend upon prophetic models – unless we argue, as has been recently done, that the act of canonizing the Bible has included an editorial process of turning disparate figures into more conventional prophetic ones.

But there are other frameworks that we recurrently recognize. Israel's covenant with God is perhaps the most powerful metaphor for their ongoing relationship – a contractual obligation, binding

upon both partners. Within that covenant, the disasters that befall
the people are frequently described to conform with the ancient list
of curses at the end of the books of Leviticus and Deuteronomy,
which are the sanctions of the covenant, the 'small print' at the
bottom of the contract.

The prophets work within a tradition of law that also belongs to
the covenantal requirements so that Jeremiah, for example, can use
the instance of a householder's right to self-defence when catching a
thief breaking in as a model for condemning the injustice perpe-
trated by the rich against the innocent poor. Their blood has been
shed with no legal justification, they were not even caught breaking
in (Jer. 2.34).

Even the reluctance of the prophets to accept their call from God
seems to belong at least to a literary convention – with different
prophets giving different accounts of how their reluctance was
overcome.

From the stories of Moses' encounters with Pharaoh we have the
most explicit description of one major task of the prophet. God tells
Moses: I have appointed you as 'God' to Pharaoh and Aaron your
brother will be your 'prophet' – you will speak all that I command
you and Aaron your brother will speak to Pharaoh (Ex. 7.1–2).
Against a 'divine' Pharaoh, God sets up a 'divine' Moses whose
mysterious instructions are to be conveyed by his official representative. This passage belongs to the ironic theme of the undermining
of Pharaoh's pretensions and hubris in taking on the real God, but
the function of the prophet as God's spokesman is clear.

Again Moses is the model for another key role to be played by the
prophet, that of intercessor on behalf of the people before their
God. After the golden calf and after the episode of the spies and the
people's refusal to enter the promised land, Moses stands in the
breach, pleading with God not to destroy the people and thus defeat
the divine experiment with Abraham and his successors which has
at stake the preservation of God's entire world. Moses even resists
the temptation to be the physical founder of a renewed people, a
second Abraham. In a dramatic reversal of this convention,
Jeremiah is told by God not to intercede on behalf of the people –
their crime is so great that God does not wish to save them any
more. The tragedy of Jeremiah is to find himself knowing that
destruction will come and praying to God to avert it despite God's
prohibition, and at the same time being condemned by the very
people he is defending because of the warnings of doom that he

gives them. Perhaps it is this paradoxical situation that leads Jeremiah to use additional images for the prophet. He is the watchman set on a tower to warn of the arrival of the enemy (Jer. 6.17 cf. Ezek. 3.16–21; 33.1–9); and when no one pays heed to his warning then he is to be a gleaner (6.9) seeking the few righteous people who follow God's ways or the assayer (6.27) seeking silver among the base metal but finding none.

What we see here may be a radicalization of the prophetic role, or perhaps a proper expression of its original purpose. The prophet is to be a constant reminder of the deepest of all of Israel's obligations – not to material prosperity or to military prowess or any other of the conventional standards of national or public success, but to a qualify of life that bears witness to the will of the God who brought them out from slavery to freedom to create a new kind of society, and ultimately to bring the world back to the unity and harmony it knew in Eden.

There are enormous possibilities for conflict of opinion within the area of prediction, of divine revelation, of the interpretation of visions and dreams. Presumably within the framework of the prophetic tradition lie disciplines, studies and experimentation in the obtaining of such revelatory experiences and their interpretations. The only direct evidence we have of this is in the music that accompanied the wandering prophets that Saul encountered. The rigorous condemnation in the Bible of wizards, necromancers, soothsayers and all who used familiar spirits and other forms of divination would suggest, at its crudest level, a rigorous trade-unionism in defining who could authentically be employed to consult God about the future (whether within priestly or prophetic traditions), and a conscious exclusion of the practices and practitioners from surrounding cultures and societies. But alongside this is also a deep awareness of the problematic of going beyond the knowledge available to the senses and to reason, and in general in the Bible a constant exclusion of magic or any source of power other than God.

Undoubtedly the prophetic tradition includes the element of prediction of future events on both a local and a grand scale. Prophets are summoned by the king to tell the outcome of a war, what is God's will in the matter? Samuel the seer is asked where Saul's donkeys are to be located, and will predict the encounters Saul will have in the next few days. Jeremiah has intuitions of the imminent arrival of 'the enemy from the North' whose precise

identity for many years is obscure to him, but whose coming and
whose overwhelming destructive power is certain. He will also
predict with uncomfortable precision the death of his opponent
Hananiah. But the element of prediction is not the essential
hallmark of the classical prophets. Rather it is the conditional
reading of events that is important – if you do not change your ways
then God will inevitably bring about this form of punishment.
Which suggests that the significance of the prophet lies not so much
in his foreseeing the future as in his analysis of the present – of his
ability to see below the surface of events to what is really going on,
in terms of a moral and religious standard that his contemporaries
have managed to shut out from their consciousness. Nor is this a
purely intellectual exercise – though with figures like Isaiah one has
more of a feeling of a rigorous intelligence at work in his analysing
of the faults of his society. Rather we feel the workings of a sensitive
intuition acting on a preconscious level, at least in the initial impact
of the revelation.

Hosea finds in the troubled and tangled emotional interrelationship with his unfaithful wife the feelings and reactions of God when
confronted with a wayward Israel, lurching back and forth between
love and hatred, overwhelming sympathy and bitter feelings of
betrayal. Jeremiah walks through the streets of Jerusalem and in his
ears there sounds the whole time the blast of the horn, warning of
the approach of an enemy – a sound that he alone can hear and to
which everyone else is stunningly indifferent. He hears a woman
crying out as if in childbirth, gasping for breath – the sound of Zion
in the throes of destruction. In the crowded streets he hears at times
only silence, the silence of death when there is no more to be heard
'the sound of mirth and the sound of gladness, the voice of the
bridegroom and the voice of the bride' (Jer. 7.34). 'If I go out into
the field, behold, those slain by the sword. And, if I enter the city,
behold, the diseases of famine' (Jer. 14.18).

Each will search within his society for the particular failures that
have led to this condemnation by God. For Amos, with the rise of a
new land-owning class, it is the blatant injustice done to the poor,
dispossessing them from their ancestral lands, that must be
attacked. Jeremiah sees in the syncretistic worship of other gods a
crime against God and the covenant. Many of them, including
Isaiah and Amos, will see a disastrous complacency in their
religious life, whereby the lavish fulfilment of sacrificial worship is
used as an evasion of ethical responsibilities. Though here we must

mention a major problem – namely that the extreme richness and complexity of their language and its frequent obscurity of terminology or allusion hides from us time and again the exact implications of their attacks. They are speaking to their own people about both contemporary and timeless issues. To their words we are eavesdroppers. The desperate importance to their followers of these writings, that led to the desire to preserve them as the central and essential documents of their past, gives a poignancy to the Hebrew Bible and an unnerving awareness of what can no longer be deciphered and of what warnings we may be as unable to heed as were the prophets' contemporaries. Which leads us to one of the central problems of biblical prophecy and the brief episode recorded in the Book of Jeremiah about his encounter with the prophet Hananiah. For in a world of authenticated prophets, each giving contradictory readings of God's will, whom do we believe?

Attempts at a formal solution are offered in the Book of Deuteronomy, within which comes the promise that there will be successors to Moses, other prophets to guide the people. 'And if you say in your heart: How may we know the word which the Eternal has not spoken? When a prophet speaks in the name of the Eternal, if the word does not come to pass or come true, that is a word which the Eternal has not spoken; the prophet has spoken it presumptuously, you need not be afraid of him' (Deut. 18.21–22). But how can we know at the time of the prophecy whether it will come true or not: And anyway, is mere predictive ability evidence of a divine word?

Moses has already utilized a 'sign' as a way of indicating the future. How will Israel know that God was indeed sent him to get them to the promised land? The sign will be that they will meet God at Sinai after they leave Egypt. That is to say, the short-term sign, once proven, is evidence that the long-term prediction will also come true. But this criterion is no less problematic, as the other legislation in Deuteronomy (13.2–4) points out: 'If a prophet arises among you, or a dreamer of dreams, and gives you a sign or a wonder, and the sign or wonder which he tells you comes to pass, and if he says: "Let us go after other gods", which you have not known, "and let us serve them", you shall not listen to the words of that prophet or to that dreamer of dreams; for the Eternal your God is testing you, to know whether you love the Eternal your God with all your heart and with all your soul.' We are firmly pushed back upon ourselves to gauge the nature of the prophet's words and not be misled by his ability to predict or perform minor miracles.

It is time to test these criteria out in the battle between Jeremiah
and Hananiah. The time is about ten years before the destruction of
Jerusalem. The previous king of Judah in allying himself with
Egypt, the other major world power of his time, had refused to pay
his regular tribute to his Babylonian masters. As a punishment
Jerusalem was attacked, the king's successor taken into captivity in
Babylon along with the elite of the ruling class and the temple
treasures. A puppet king was installed on the throne. In response to
this affront to national pride, patriotic elements in Judah felt it
necessary to revolt against Babylon and were encouraged in this by
Egyptian promises of help. Against this political turmoil, it must
have been difficult for Jeremiah's contemporaries to separate the
religious from the political elements in his message. He preached
submission to Nebuchadnezzar, king of Babylon. He saw the
actions of Babylon as being God's deliberate punishment of His
errant people for their corruption and failure.

Thus religiously he was going against the triumphalism that so
often goes along with religious loyalties. Politically he must have
been standing directly in the face of the hurt pride and nationalistic
fervour of his contemporaries and indeed international alliances
and shifting alignments between the two superpowers that domin-
ated the region. When envoys from several local nations came to
Jerusalem to suggest to King Zedekiah that they unite against the
common enemy Babylon, Jeremiah was instructed to make a yoke
and wear it about his neck and proclaim to the visiting emissaries the
message of the Lord.

> It is I who by my great power and my outstretched arm have made
> the earth, with the men and animals that are on the earth, and I
> give it to whomever it seems right to me. Now I have given all
> these lands into the hand of Nebuchadnezzar, the king of
> Babylon, my servant, and I have given him also the beasts of the
> field to serve him. All the nations shall serve him and his son and
> his grandson, until the time of his own land comes, then many
> nations and great kings shall make him their slave. But if any
> nation or kingdom will not serve this Nebuchadnezzar king of
> Babylon and put its neck under the yoke of the king of Babylon, I
> will punish that nation with the sword, with famine, and with
> pestilence, says the Eternal, until I have consumed it by his hand.
> So do not listen to your prophets, your diviners, your dreamers,
> your soothsayers, or your sorcerers, who are saying to you, 'You

shall not serve the king of Babylon'. For it is a lie which they are prophesying to you, with the result that you will be removed far from your land, and I will drive you out and you will perish (Jer. 27.5–10).

Jeremiah brought a similar message to King Zedekiah and to the priests. He also accused the prophets of not fulfilling their responsibilities. Nebuchadnezzar, says Jeremiah, will remove all the rest of the sacred vessels of the Temple to Babylon, and the prophets should be interceding with God to prevent this happening, not prophesying Nebuchadnezzar's defeat. Against this challenging background comes the debate within the Temple precincts, in the presence of the priests and the people, between Jeremiah and Hananiah the prophet, presumably representing the official prophetic view. Two figures of tremendous spiritual authority are standing in the central religious and national shrine arguing before the leaders of their society about the will of God in their time – and at stake is the destiny of the nation. Hananiah with all the power and authority of his position, and presumably reinforced by the presence within the city of the foreign emissaries and the royal backing for a policy of revolt, is the first to speak.

Thus says the Eternal of hosts, the God of Israel: I have broken the yoke of the king of Babylon. Within two years I will bring back to this place all the vessels of the Eternal's house, which Nebuchadnezzar king of Babylon took away from this place and carried to Babylon. I will also bring back to this place Jeconiah the son of Jehoiakim, king of Judah, and all the exiles from Judah who went to Babylon, says the Eternal, for I will break the yoke of the king of Babylon (Jer. 28.2).

How could one doubt such sentiments? Their language is the language of prophecy, their authority comes from God himself, and the sentiments accord with every intuitive feeling and innermost need and desire of the people themselves. To Jeremiah it can only seem as wishful thinking. In his long critique of the prophets (in chapter 23) he characterizes their words: 'they fill you with vain ideas; it is a vision from their own mind they speak, not something from the mouth of God. They say continually to those who despise the word of God: "All will be well with you", and to those who walk in the stubbornness of their own heart they say: "No harm shall come to you"' (13.16f.).

It is the banality of their words, their self-seeking nature, that
offends Jeremiah – for he has experienced God as an overwhelming
force. 'Is not my word like fire, says the Eternal, and like a hammer
which breaks the rock in pieces' (23.29). But these practitioners
have no sense of that power: 'They have healed the wound of my
people lightly, saying: "Peace, peace" – but there is no peace!'
(6.13). Their complacency is summed up in the language not only of
the prophets but of the priesthood with their magical reliance on the
Temple to save them whatever they do. 'Do not trust these false
words, saying: The Temple of the Eternal, the Temple of the
Eternal, the Temple of the Eternal!' (7.4).

Yet Martin Buber sees Hananiah as a patriot, convinced that
'Jeremiah had no love whatsoever for his country, for if he had, how
could he have expected his people to bend their necks to the yoke?'
'Hananiah considered himself a great politician, for he thought that
in an hour of danger he had succeeded in strengthening the people's
resistance. But what he actually strengthened was an illusion,
which, when it collapsed, would cause the collapse of the people's
strength. Jeremiah, on the other hand, wanted to protect Israel
from just that. The only way to salvation is by the steep and stony
path over the recognition of reality'.[1]

Jeremiah's reply to Hananiah is unexpectedly mild. He says:
'Amen, so may it be! May the Eternal do so; may the Eternal make
the words which you have prophesied come true and bring back to
this place from Babylon the vessels of the House of the Eternal and
all the exiles'. But having expressed this wish he brings in yet
another attempt to refine the problem of how to recognize the
genuineness of a prophet. 'The prophets who preceded you and me
from ancient times prophesied war, famine and pestilence against
many countries and great kingdoms. As for the prophet who
prophesies peace, when the word of that prophet comes to pass,
then it will be known that the Eternal has truly sent the prophet.'

Prophets, he argues, are there to warn, not to bless the *status quo*.
It is a powerful argument for it evokes the sense of dread and
wonder at the thought that God can address human beings, and
conjures up the pictures of a long tradition of prophetic figures who
acted as critics to their society. It even belongs to a current acceptance of the dissident prophet as debated in Jeremiah's public trial
some years before, recorded in chapter 26 of his book. Perhaps his

[1]Martin Buber, *Biblical Humanism*, London 1968, p. 169.

argument even swayed the people, because Hananiah was forced to take drastic action. He snatched the yoke off Jeremiah's neck and broke it: 'Thus says the Eternal. Even so will I break the yoke of Nebuchadnezzar king of Babylon from the neck of all the nations within two years'. And Jeremiah is silent – he has no instant word from God with which to answer, Hananiah has won the debate and Jeremiah must leave.

There is a subtle ploy of the author of this passage. Throughout he uses the title 'prophet' after the name of each of the protagonists, until here. When Hananiah speaks these words he speaks as Hananiah, not as Hananiah the prophet. And perhaps that hint to the reader is the only clue available to the onlookers with which to judge the truth of what he says. Buber tries to characterize the two men at this moment:

(Jeremiah) was silent when the bar was broken and went his way. He went in order to listen for God's word. Why did he go? Obviously, because in spite of everything there were still things he did not know. Hananiah had spoken like a man who 'knows it all'. Jeremiah had heard him speak like a man who 'knows it all', but there were still things Jeremiah himself did not know. God had, indeed, spoken to him only an hour before. But this was another hour. History is a dynamic process, and history means that one hour is never like the one that has gone before. God operates in history, and God is not a machine which, once it has been wound up, keeps on running until it runs down. He is a living God. Even the word God speaks at a certain hour, the word one obeys by laying a yoke on one's neck, must not be hung up like a placard . . . One must not rely on one's knowledge. One must go one's way and listen all over again . . . Hananiah 'knew it all', He did not know the truth, because he 'knew it all'.[2]

Hananiah wins the debate and Jeremiah is beaten – because a popular mood required simpler, more reassuring messages and more successful heroes. It was only later that a defeated people could remember and canonize the words of the man they scorned, imprisoned, and as legend has it, eventually murdered in Egyptian exile. Yet we must be careful not to fall into the trap of reading in Jeremiah's fate some ultimate criterion for evaluating the biblical prophet. Others, according to the record, were listened to and

[2] *Biblical Humanism*, pp. 166f.

catastrophe averted (Jer. 26.18–19). Nor is the gloominess of the prediction the necessary proof of its authenticity, despite Jeremiah's own words. Jeremiah the passionate critic of his people in their complacency, becomes the messenger of hope, renewal and restoration to the broken nation and the exiles in Babylon – though his message to them of waiting in exile for God to bring them back and pray for the peace of the land of their captivity was no less disturbing to those who still put a limited national pride above the greater will of their God.

The very unpredictability of the prophetic word should warn us that the immediate political or social constellations are not for them the ultimate matter at issue. Though it is an uncomfortable thought, it is not futurology, whether optimistic or pessimistic, that is at stake. It is not political decisions or forms of government that may be important, for biblical Israel lived under many kinds of regime, as an independent nation and under foreign rule. It is not, strange to say, the question of militarism, though the prophets saw in armaments absurd things in which to put ultimate hopes. In all these and other matters that are crucial for our survival, what counted for the biblical prophets was an individual and collective commitment to the covenant, to a transcendent reality that demanded submission to a will greater than human, and hence a necessary humility. That was Jeremiah's humility in leaving the debating chamber rather than try to bluff his way like Hananiah, and thus claim to control the word of God. From the pride of the builders of the Tower of Babel, to the Babylonian king attacked by Isaiah for claiming to set his throne in the heavens, it is the hubris that makes human beings set themselves above their creator which leads to divine intervention and disaster.

How we translate such a lesson from its Israelite origins in a God-centred world to a secular one is another matter. Hubris is easy to recognize, if no less difficult to combat – in others as well as in ourselves. Compared to the Assyrians and Babylonians feared by biblical Israel our own superpower politics seem no less grotesque threatening and beyond control. Jeremiah could also envision a world returning to the chaos and void prior to creation, without cities, without vegetation, without creatures, without human beings, and fear its imminent arrival (Jer. 4.23–26). Amos could see the exploitation and enslavement of the poor, reinforced by a corrupt social and legal system against which no redress was possible. Isaiah could see a religion that was an opiate, not for the suffering poor as Marx understood it, but for the complacent rich. Jeremiah could detect in the corruption of the language used by the prophets evidence of corruption within. There are no lack of analogies – the problem lies in how we respond to them.

I wrote at the beginning of the inevitable failure of the prophets. The paradox of their lives, as Jonah was to experience, was that if they succeeded in transmitting the word of God effectively, they became at that very moment redundant. But the fate of the biblical prophets was more often that they failed to reach their contemporaries – and only those who came after, with the wisdom of hindsight, could see the truth of what they said. The trouble is that mechanically translating their vision into a contemporary situation is equally fallacious – for history, the world and God have moved on. Because they failed in their own time because people did not wish to see beyond the comfortable surface they can teach us to be wary of the conventional wisdom, received traditions and fashionable truths of our own time. But also there may be something to learn from the wisdom of a David. The classical prophet was part of a triumvirate of powers that must live in dynamic tension with each other, providing a whole series of checks and balances against the overwhelming authority of any single one of them. Unbridled political power, unself-critical religious control or a prophetic zeal that knows no compromise with human weakness are equally disastrous to human survival.

The prophet as the loyal opposition in our society is to be searched out, listened and responded to – provided we do not neglect at the same time to strengthen the authority and self-corrective powers of government and the discipline and self-purification of our religious traditions. But on another level, the prophet is also our dreamer of dreams who brings us the vision of what might yet be. To him or her we owe images of restoration and rebirth, of hope and reconciliation; of a humanity restored to unity, of the harmony of animal and human beings, and of a world without fear. These visions are always beyond the horizon, for the watchman on his tower can only see with growing dread the arrival of the foe. Without this vision we are condemned to a world without meaning or hope, but with it we might survive, yet again, the onslaught of our own self-mutilation.

— 13 —

Images of God

While preparing this chapter a verse occurred to me which became the inevitable starting point. It comes from Solomon's speech at the dedication of the Temple: 'Behold the heavens and the heaven of heavens cannot contain You, how much less so this Temple that I have built.' (I Kings 8.27). How much less can this brief chapter do justice to the concept of God in the Hebrew Bible! But I do not think that Solomon was merely stating the obvious, nor being unduly modest. Clearly the Temple could not contain God, but it could give the reassurance that the presence of God could be found and encountered. Or is the reverse the case? It has been argued by Robert Van Pelt (at a lecture delivered at the fifteenth Jewish-Christian Bible Week in Bendorf) that Temples serve the opposite function:

> In archaic cultures, like the Israelite in the time of Solomon, the problems man faced in his relation with the divine, the supernatural, were quite different from ours. We desperately try to find the imprints of God in a secularized society. Archaic man did not have to search for it: the numinous was everywhere. Each tree, each well, each mountain or hill had its spirit, belonged to a god, all of whom demanded honour, respect and attention. The problem archaic man faced was how to create in this world a kind of free-haven, where he would be free from the unbearable burden which the gods imposed on the shoulders of man.
>
> Almost all cultures have found a way out, have been able to shake off, at least in daily life, the yoke of the supernatural cosmos. And the way they did so has been virtually the same all over the world: one created a special place which was designated to carry the burden, 'liberating' the remaining

space. This special place, which was set apart was the so-called 'holy place'.

If our problem is the apparent absence of God, the Israelite's problem was the overwhelming presence of God. If our problem is the struggle to find a suitable image of God for our times, the problem of the biblical period is the superabundance of gods, and indeed images of Israel's God, with which they had to contend. The designations and names, borrowed from local Canaanite practice and suitably modified, as well as the images and metaphors created by Israel, never cease to flow from the pages of the Bible: *El, El Shaddai, El Elyon, El Roi, El Berith, El Olam, El Elohai Yisrael, Elohim, Eloah*; *Pachad Yitzhak* (the Fear of Isaac), *Abir Ya'akov* (the Mighty One of Jacob), *Ha Tzur* (the Rock), the Eternal (Lord) of Hosts, King, Judge, Shepherd, Father, the Holy One, Redeemer; the living God, the Ancient of Days. They testify to a multiplicity of traditions, and behind them a multiplicity of experiences, cherished, handed on and interpreted throughout the generations – and somehow recognized, despite their enormous diversity of nature and origin, as reflecting in some way a unity, a oneness, that lies behind them.

The God of the Hebrew Bible is called 'One' in the famous formulation of Deuteronomy 6.4, 'Hear O Israel, the Eternal our God, the Eternal is One'. Yet this oneness, this unity, this uniqueness, comes to us through multifarious images, through terms that describe and through terms that conceal. Between us and that God stand many layers of camouflage and confusion.

The limits of human language make impossible a description of what is, by definition, both indescribable and indefinable. And the very attempts of our Hebrew ancestors to depict God are even further confounded for us by our own distance in time and space from their culture, language and perceptions. Even if we knew the language and what it really signified, between the record we have inherited and the 'truth' about God stand the limitations of the human witnesses to the divine. Between what the biblical narrators and poets experienced and recorded and the reality that underlay it is an enormous gap, one that they themselves recognized. Ezekiel saw 'the appearance of the likeness of the glory of the Eternal' (1.28). Hosea tells us that God has 'spoken to the prophets and multiplied visions and through the prophets given parables' (12.11). Elijah learnt that God was not in the storm, nor

in the earthquake, nor in the fire, but in the sound of utter silence
(I Kings 19.11–12).

All these are human attempts to describe what cannot be
described. And that is assuming we can trust these human witnesses in the first place. But prophets are notoriously unreliable,
sometimes preferring to give words of comfort or convenience
rather than words of truth. Jeremiah fought such false prophets'
use of technical prophetic terminology to present their own ideas,
those who 'oracularize oracles' to capture his own coinage of their
actions (*vayin'amu n'oom*) (Jer. 23.32). And even the 'good'
prophets, the ones we trust, can get it wrong. It is not just that
prophecy is conditional, so that human actions can change destiny
– sometimes their own judgment is at fault. So that much play is
made of Samuel picking the wrong son of Jesse to anoint as King
(I Sam. 16.6) – chosen because of his size, just like the fated Saul.
'For', says God, 'it is not as man sees; for man looks on the
outward appearance but the Lord looks on the heart.' Samuel who
is called the 'seer' (I Sam. 9.9) is ironically the one who does not
'see'. The Bible itself tells us that our witnesses are flawed, our
vision imperfect and our ability to communicate it limited – so we
must be very wary in any assertion we make about the 'God of the
Hebrew Bible'.

God, too, is evasive. The patriarchs seem to take for granted
both the reality and nature of the God they encounter. True,
Abraham explores the parameters of God's sense of justice in his
argument about Sodom, but Moses seems to be the first to try to
pin down something of the qualities and nature of God. His first
attempt at the burning bush receives what is both a revelation and
at the same time a clear rebuff. To his request to know God's
name comes the famous, if untranslatable, *ehyeh asher enyeh*: 'I
am what I am', or 'I will be what I will be', or any number of
variations on that sort of construction. As we have already noted,
there are numerous theological and philosophical attempts to
grasp the implications of this statement that relates, at least in its
language, to the verb 'to be', 'to exist' – perhaps implying God's
timelessness or existential presence. Nevertheless the grammatical
form is similar to other constructions that are actually evasive. So
that when we are not to know where David's men spent some
time, we are told: 'they went where they went' (I Sam. 23.13). 'I
am what I am' can mean: you cannot contain my nature within the
framework of a name, and thus, in some sense, have power over

me as do others who know the name of their god. I am ultimately only to be understood in my own terms. I am what I am. In other words: 'Mind your own business!'

If that seems rather harsh, it is no less problematic than God's initial response to Moses' second attempt to learn something of the nature of God's ways. After the episode of the Golden Calf, when the whole enterprise seems lost, Moses must plead with God for his continued presence in the midst of the people. Emboldened by God's positive response, he asks 'Show me your Glory.' Already we have problems with the term *kavod*, translated as 'glory', which can mean 'honour' or 'glory', but also can stand for the concept of 'person', 'self', much as the word 'name'. In reply God promises to pass his 'goodness' before Moses – and this would seem to mean from the subsequent passage where God spells out his own qualities: compassion and mercy, patience and faithful loyalty or love, that lasts a thousand generations, forgiving all kinds of wrongdoing, but not letting the guilty go unpunished' (Ex. 34.6–7). But at the moment of his initial answer God adds (Ex. 33.19) – 'but I will be gracious to whom I will be gracious, and show mercy to whom I show mercy', which is a similar grammatical construction to the one we have just seen: I am what I am and I do what I like!

An anarchic power remains within God in his ultimate rule of the world. That is to say, in terms of God's very nature (his 'name') and his dealings with humanity (his 'glory') God retires behind mystery and seeming arbitrariness. If God could be defined, was predictable and thus manipulable, he would cease to be God. Yet that God allows himself to be bound by a covenant with a certain people, thus seemingly limiting his power. The first of many paradoxes we shall meet.

To return again to the problem of the biblical witness itself, we are today ever more conscious of the nature of the record before us and the new perspective this gives us of the stories it contains. For example the encounter at the burning bush is only one of a number of similar stories which share common terminology and features. I have mentioned above that an identical word play exists at the beginning of Exodus 3, the burning bush, and Genesis 18, Abraham's encounter with the three 'angels'.[1] In both, a variation on the use of the verb 'to see', allows us to view the same story through the 'objective' eyes of the narrator and the 'subjective' eyes of the

[1]'The Bush that Never Burnt: Narrative Techniques in Exodus 3 and 6', *Heythrop Journal*, vol. XVI, 3, July 1975, pp. 304–11.

participant in the drama. Moses sees a bush burning, but we, the readers, know there is an angel standing in it. Abraham sees three men, *we* know it is really God manifesting Himself through them. The same literary device is applied with Gideon's encounter with the angel and with the angel who appears to Samson's mother. But these angels/messengers/men also appear to Joshua before his first battle, to Jacob who wrestles with one and to Hagar lost in the desert.

When we read that Joseph, wandering around looking for his brothers, meets a man who sends him off to find them with some cryptic remarks, we wait for this man, too, to turn into an angel – when he does not, we realize that this is yet another variation on the theme, possibly indicating that Joseph at this stage in his life cannot see beyond the surface appearance of events. That is to say, these different episodes are variations on a particular 'type-scene' (to use Robert Alter's terminology[2]) – They are a narrative convention in which the art lies in providing particular variations on the basic theme appropriate to the context.

We have become conscious of the artistic control that lies between the original experience, its transmission and its final telling (apart from questions of later editing and canonization). We have gained in recognizing the subtlety and complexity behind the apparent simplicity or naivety of the stories – our biblical ancestors are neither 'primitive' nor uneducated nor unsophisticated. But we have lost out in our own simple identification with the stories themselves as divine 'truth'. One of the recurrent themes in this particular set of stories, except the Joseph one where we can argue it is deliberately suppressed, is both the wonder at the encounter with God in whatever manifestation, and the teasing, often overtly humorous, nature of the narrative itself. We laugh at the expense of our heroes – even Moses – and become conscious yet again of the distance between God and humanity, and the impossibility of expressing all but the merest hint of God's reality. We settle instead for a wide variety of expressions of that distance itself.

In fact the irony that is so frequently expressed in the Hebrew Bible repeatedly points to many such incongruities: to the distance between our perception of ourselves and God's knowledge of the reality of human life; to our sense of our own power and God's awareness of our weakness. Irony becomes the literary device which makes palatable, even bearable, this enormous dissonance

[2]Robert Alter, *The Art of Biblical Narrative*, Allen & Unwin 1981, pp. 47–62.

between our seemingly limitless human gifts, powers and creativity that makes us 'little less than divine' (Ps. 8.5) and our human frailty – for we are like 'grass that grows in the morning, that grows so fresh in the morning, and in the evening fades and dies' (Ps. 90.5–6).

Yet having recognized the art and craftsmanship that moulds our perception of events and brings with it a certain detachment, we are also conscious among the biblical witnesses of those for whom the experience of God was so overwhelming as to be almost tangible – whether intoxicating in its awesome excitement or devastating in its unrelenting dread. Jeremiah could experience both, as expressed in his subtle 'confessions'. 'Your words were found and I ate them, and your words became to me a joy and the delight of my heart, for I am called by your name, O Eternal, God of hosts.' (Jer. 15.16). 'For the word of the Eternal has become for me a reproach and derision all day long. If I say, "I will not mention him, or speak any more in his name", there is in my heart as it were a burning fire shut up in my bones, and I am weary with holding it in, and I cannot' (Jer. 20.8b–9).

More savage and sarcastic is Job who takes the cherished phrases of his tradition and turns them inside out. The Psalmist can ask with wonder, as we have already quoted:

What is man that you are mindful of him, and the son of man that you care for him? Yet you have made him little less than divine, and crown him with glory and honour (Ps. 8.5).

In Job's bitter experience the words become:

What is man that You make so much of him, that You pay such close attention to him? that You visit him every morning, testing him every single moment!?! (Job 7.17–18).

In Jonah's paranoid universe, every breath of wind, every creature, every plant, every human word echoes with the demanding insistence that he do God's will and go against his own common sense and desires to the wicked city of Nineveh, God is manifestly there, close, too close, and, in the phrase of the Rabbis, 'the Master of the House is urgent!'

Yet, as Jeremiah also testified, when needed, God had the uncomfortable habit of disappearing; silent, seemingly unmoved by the suffering of His spokesman, and indeed of His people, as Israel was to testify time after time. The poem in Deuteronomy 32 has God, angry at Israel's abandoning of Him, threatening also to disappear, saying: 'I will hide My face from them' (Deut. 32.20, compare Deut. 31.18). Time and again in the Bible we find a tantalizing game of hide and seek between human beings and God. One of the writers of the Psalms can speak of his own age that 'this is the generation of those that seek him, those who seek Your face are Jacob' (Ps. 24.6). Yet the writer we know as Third Isaiah, can have God lament: 'I was ready to be sought by those who did not ask. I was ready to be found by those who did not seek. I said "Here am I", "Here am I" to a nation that did not call on my name' (Isa. 65.1).

It is part of a tragi-comedy, all too human in its expression, yet acted out on a cosmic scale. From the very beginning of Genesis, God is portrayed as a tragic hero, whose attempts to obtain the loyalty and love of his creatures, his beloved, constantly end in disappointment, frustration, anger and retribution – to be followed by tearful reconciliations. In Heschel's phrase God is 'in search of man'.

It is yet another paradox of the biblical picture that such an anthropomorphic image can predominate alongside theological attempts to insist upon the otherness of God. Isaiah (chapter 6) sets side by side the transcendence of God (Holy, holy, holy – i.e. 'separate' and 'other' beyond human imagining) and God's immanence – the earth is filled with his *kavod*, glory, presence.[3] Or the warning in Deuteronomy (4.15–18):

> Therefore take good heed to yourself. Since you saw no form on the day that the Eternal spoke to you at Horeb out of the midst of the fire, beware lest you act corruptly by making a graven image for yourselves in the form of any figure, the likeness of male or female, the likeness of any beast that is on the earth, the likeness of any winged bird that flies in the air, the likeness of anything that creeps on the ground, the likeness of any fish that is in the water under the earth.

It is not just that God is greater than the other gods, as is asserted in the Song at the Sea (Ex. 15.11), 'Who is like you, Eternal, among the gods? Who, like you, is majestic in holiness, awesome in praise, working wonders?' But God, for Second Isaiah, is unique: 'I am the first and I am the last; besides me there is no god' (Isa. 44.6). 'I am the Eternal and there is no other, beside me there is no god. I gird

[3]For a more detailed discussion of this passage see my article 'A Little Lower than the Angels' in *Harvest: Journal for Jungian Studies*, 28, 1982, pp. 97–105.

you though you do not know me' (Isa. 45.5). 'For I am God and there is no other, I am God and there is none like me' (Isa. 46.9). That insistent voice is both demanding and pathetic at one and the same time.

Yet again and again this God who is transcendent, distant and remote is concerned with the minutest details of human experience and life. For Jeremiah God's geographical starting point in the following passage is heaven to which God might be considered 'near', and thus 'far' from human life.

> Am I a God who stays near at hand, says the Lord, and not a God in the far distance? Can a man hide himself in secret places so that I cannot see him? says the Eternal. Do I not fill heaven *and* earth? says the Eternal (Jer. 23. 23–4).

Whereas Jeremiah uses the image to point to God's awareness of the dishonesty of the false prophets on the earth, the composer of Psalm 113 uses the metaphor of God's 'height' above the earth to allow God to descend and raise to the 'heights' those who are bent low.

> High above all nations is the Eternal beyond the heavens is his glory. Who is like the Eternal our God, who lives so far beyond, who dwells so close within, to watch the heavens and the earth? He raises the weak from the dust, lifts the poor from the dirt, to set them with the noble, with the noble of his people (Psa. 113.4–8).

Which brings us back again full circle to Job's complaint that God never leaves human beings alone for a moment! And this in turn reminds us of the subjectivity of our biblical witnesses, of their humanity and hence the inevitable 'humanity' of the biblical images of God – who can 'change his mind'; who is seemingly subject to human passions, who can proclaim his compassion and love at one moment and decree the destruction of the world, or the annihilation of an enemy people, at the next. It is as mistaken to focus exclusively on the biblical God's love, justice and pity as epitomizing his nature and qualities – as religious apologists tend to do, as it is to focus on his anger and destructiveness and seeming anarchic choices – as anti-religious apologists do. Either they are all there or none are there. Without such a totality, without such contradictions, God would not be God. 'I form light and create darkness. I form peace and create evil. I the Eternal do all these things' (Isa. 45.7).

It is one of the features of the biblical record that people are often wrong about God, Israel no less, perhaps even more so, than other nations. 'God is on our side and will destroy our enemies', say Amos' contemporaries. To which the prophet must reply:

> Woe to you who desire the day of the Eternal! Why would you have the day of the Eternal? It is darkness and not light (Amos 5.18).

'God can be appeased by the proper functioning of our rituals, the marvellous richness of our services and our sacrifices.'

> I hate, I despise your feasts, and I take no delight in your solemn assemblies. Even though you offer me your burnt offerings and cereal offerings, I will not accept them, and the peace offerings of your fatted beasts I will not look upon. Take away from me the noise of your songs; to the melody of your harps I will not listen. But let justice roll down like waters and righteousness like an ever-flowing stream (Amos 5.21–24).

'We are God's chosen people and only our destiny is linked to him!'

> Are you not like the Ethiopians to me, O children of Israel?', says the Eternal. 'Did I not bring up Israel from the land of Egypt, and the Philistines from Caphtor and the Syrians from Kir? (Amos 9.7).

'Because God loves us in a special way he will always guard and protect us, come what may.'

> You only have I known of all the families of the earth; therefore I will pay particularly close attention to your wrongdoings! (Amos 3.2).

For Isaiah at a certain moment in time the threat of an enemy besieging Jerusalem is not important – God will preserve his city. And Isaiah is right. For Jeremiah, a century later, that same Jerusalem will assuredly be destroyed by the Babylonians – despite the faith of his contemporaries, reinforced by Isaiah's teaching, that God will never allow it to fall. And Jeremiah too is right. It is as if God refuses to be taken for granted. That no two situations are ever the same. That history, tradition or simple faith offer no guarantee for the present. Either God's word is alive, and present, and demanding to be heard – or it is not. And all too often that living word demands of the hearer the very opposite of what he expects. To follow the image of Jonah, Israel is forever being sent to Nineveh and being caught sneaking off to Tarshish. It is yet another paradox that for all the biblical insistence on God's justice and reliability. His loyalty to the covenant – the Bible is also a celebration of his limitless powers to surprise, not to say shock, his people into new challenges, new awarenesses, new responsibilities. 'Great is the Eternal, and much to be praised, and his greatness is unsearchable!' (Ps. 145.3).

There is no 'concept' of God in the Hebrew Bible. At best there may be 'concepts' and more appropriately we should speak of experiences, personal and collective, expressed in the widest range of literary media by innumerable generations over a considerable period of time – these experiences interacting with one another with all the resonances, contradictions and wonderment that such rich variety can give. From Moses' enthusiasm to Jacob's subtlety, from Job's bitterness to Kohelet's cynicism, from the ecstasy of the Song of Songs to the deep pain and sorrow of Lamentations, from the clarity of innumerable law-givers to the desperate search for words of the prophets, from the buffoonery of a Samson to the simplicity of a Hannah, the record is endless, the images and experiences inexhaustible and unfathomable.

The God of the Hebrew Bible lives for us because of these frail human witnesses – flawed, inadequate though they may be. Indeed they seem chosen because of their very flaws and inadequacies, and may be further maimed by the experience. They no longer live, but through them and the record they left, we have, if not a concept of God, at least our own tantalizing glimpse and experience of that power that shaped their lives, their history and their destiny. That record stimulates and challenges us still today, and just as urgently demands our response.

— 14 —

All Having Been Said

Of course there is more to say. The Rabbis point out that many of the confessions of sin that are read in the Synagogue on the Day of Atonement are arranged in the form of an alphabetical acrostic. Presumably this is an *aide memoire* from a time before written texts were readily available to the worshippers. But they derived even from this a nice interpretation. The number of sins people might conceivably commit is limitless. So people could be confessing them forever. Fortunately, however, there is a limit to the length of the alphabet so even confession has to stop at some time. There is also a limit to the length of a book.

In concluding I would like to address one more challenge to the Bible. There is a semi-religious, semi-superstitious view that when you have a problem, the Bible will provide the answer. Just open it at random and see what advice it offers you. The trouble is that on dipping in at random, rather than the comfort you seek you are as likely to open it at a list of sacrificial offerings, symptoms of 'leprosy' or curses against some obscure ancient people. Hence the practice in some Gideon Bibles of offering a list of appropriate passages for particular situations. I have already suggested frequently that the Bible offers more questions than answers, but it may well be that a particular passage, especially one from the Psalms, will speak to our mood or pain and can offer the comfort or release that we need.

But what do we do with those bits that do not seem to speak to us at all? Again there is no simple solution. Several years ago I asked a similar question of Rabbi Adin Steinsaltz, one of the most significant contemporary Orthodox Jewish scholars, who is doing a singlehanded 'translation' of the Talmud into modern Hebrew, and now into English as well. I had been visiting some friends in Israel whose daughters were in the middle of their school-leaving exams.

They had to read and comment on some chapters in Isaiah. I had a look at the passages and was horrified to find I could make neither head nor tail of them. Eventually I began to see something of what they were about but I wondered what a couple of fifteen year olds would understand. The answer from Adin was 'probably not much'. But they were only learning them for an exam, which meant they had to know something of the vocabulary and be able to answer questions on things they had prepared. Well that was all very well for an exam, but what should we do about passages like this that were so obscure and which seemed so typical of much of prophetic literature. How did one work with them and extract some sort of meaning? His answer was that the only thing you could do was get to know them, live with them, allow them to become a part of you and perhaps one day they would speak.

I believe he is right though it is a view that goes against so much in our contemporary culture which expects instant answers and satisfactions. Living with the Bible is a long-haul operation. The initial insights can be breathtaking in their impact, but when the honeymoon is over, the Bible has to be wooed and earned over and over again if it is to speak to us. A Rabbi with the strange name of Ben Bag Bag put it this way:

> Turn it and turn it again, for everything is in it. Look into it, grow old and grey over it, and do not turn away from it for you have nothing better than this (Sayings of the Fathers 5.25).

On one occasion such an obscure 'list' came alive for me and it seems an appropriate piece with which to end. It comes from another Bendorf Bible Week sermon and the passage concerned the materials used to build the sanctuary and its contents.

I suppose I want to end with it because of its theme of the unending journey. It is one of the strange features of the Pentateuch that it ends with the children of Israel at the borders of the Promised Land, but they never actually enter. This reality is dramatized in the Synagogue by the annual cycle of readings. On the festival of '*Simhat Torah*, the 'Rejoicing in the Torah' we invite someone, the 'bridegroom of the Torah', to read the closing verses of Deuteronomy and afterwards the 'Bridegroom of Genesis' reads the opening verses of Genesis, so that the cycle begins immediately again. From the borders of the Promised Land, we return to the Creation story and begin again. This pattern is echoed in the Pilgrim Festivals which take us out of Egypt (*Pesach*, Passover), to the revelation at Sinai (*Shavuot*, Pentecost), to the wandering in the wilderness (*Sukkot*, Tabernacles), and back again to Egypt when spring comes round again. We are somehow trapped in a loop of time, endlessly repeating our symbolic journey while at the same time travelling through geography and history in the 'real' world. We live in two dimensions in constant dialogue with each other. On such a journey, the Bible is a companion, a reference point, a route map and a goad.

It is important to remember the frame. We are on a journey from a land of slavery to a land of promise. We may understand the slavery how we will – it is a place or time when our life is determined by others, perhaps by unknown forces or powers. Such is our slavery that we do not recognize it for what it is. We suffer it and fear it, but fear change even more. We are dragged unwillingly, resentful, fearful out to the wilderness.

There is a land of promise – a dream, a vision, a fantasy – enough to sustain us at times, a bitter joke at others. The reality is the wilderness. It is important to remember the frame.

We are not alone in the wilderness. We may help or hinder each other. We are reasonable people and sensible. We build our camp. We deploy our families, our tribes, our nation. We order our march. We mark and name the stages – here a place called 'bitterness', there 'the waters of strife', there 'the mountain of God'.

In the centre of our camp is our mystery, our secret. It is the force that drew us out of slavery, that drives us relentlessly on. Because it set us free we fear it, we fear its urgency, we fear the price it will demand. We have lost the security of slaves but not yet gained the freedom to be free.

We guard our mystery with care. It is our source of power. If we can control it, it may take us to our land. If we fail to contain it, it may destroy us. We celebrate and we appease. We rejoice and we watch and we wait.

We build a sanctuary. With care, precision, with skill we harness all that is ours for this work. Our intellect, our creativity, our wealth, our hands – every craft of which we are master plays its part in this work. For the journey is truly immense and the land of promise far. We pour out our hearts to build a place for our God of terrible love. Such overflowing eagerness, such gifts, more than the work could ever need. And it emerges piece by piece – each masterly part finely and joyfully wrought. Nor are we so foolish as to mistake the pieces themselves for more than they are. We celebrate how we can create, but we worship still our Creator. And we name and gather, piece by piece, our wondrous work.

    the tent and all its furnishings
    its clasps
    its boards
    its bars
    its pillars
    its sockets
    the covering of ram-skins dyed red
    and the covering of sealskins
    and the veil of the screen;
    the ark of the testimony
    and its staves and cover;
    the table, its vessels and the shewbread
    the pure candlestick with its lamps to be set in order
    and its vessels and oil for the light;
    the golden incense altar;
    the oil for anointing;
    the sweet incense
    and the screen for the door of the tent;
    the altar of bronze
    its grating of brass
    its staves and all its vessels
    the laver and the base;
    the hangings of the court
    its pillars and its sockets
    and the screen for the gate of the court
    its cords and pins
    and all the instruments of the service
    of the tabernacle of the tent of meeting.
    (Ex. 39.33–40)

We build our tabernacle for God precisely because it is so tangible, so finite. It is structure, form, clarity. It is ritual, routine, responsibility. It is tending and nurture and self-sacrifice. It is symbol and model and code. It is what forms and moulds and guarantees our identity in the wilderness. It reminds us of where we have been and where we seek to go. Yet it may also become prison, obsession or death.

Whenever the cloud was taken up from over the tabernacle the children of Israel went onward throughout all their journeys (Ex. 40.36).

Each time we take our tabernacle apart, assign the pieces, repair and renew and journey on. We preserve and change. When the cloud moves on we must follow or die in the wilderness.

For we are a rabble of former slaves, bound to one another, unwillingly on our way to a land of promise. We murmur and squabble, yet together we have built our tabernacle. And together we are watching, reluctant, bewildered, impatient, waiting for the cloud to move on.

FURTHER READING

Nehama Leibowitz, *Studies in the Pentateuch* (5 Volumes) (Studies in: *Bereshit* (Genesis); *Shemot* (Exodus); *Vayikra* (Leviticus); *Bamidbar* (Numbers); *Devarim* (Deuteronomy), The World Zionist Organization Department for Torah Education and Culture in the Diaspora, Jerusalem 1980.

Hyam Maccoby, *Judaism on Trial: Jewish-Christian Disputations in the Middle Ages*, Littman Library of Jewish Civilization, Oxford University Press 1982.